PIECES OF A SONG

Selected Poems

Diane di Prima

City Lights Books
San Francisco

© 1990 Diane di Prima

Foreword © 1973 by Robert Creeley
Reprinted by permission of Robert Creeley

Cover by Sheppard Powell

Library of Congress Cataloging-in-Publication Data

Di Prima, Diane.
    Pieces of a song : selected poems / by Diane di Prima.
      p. cm.
    ISBN 0-87286-237-2 : $10.95
    I. Title
    PS3507.I68P5 1989   89-25243
    811'.54—dc20   CIP

City Lights Books are available to bookstores through our primary
distributor: Subterranean Company, P.O. Box 10233, Eugene, OR 97440.
(503) 343-6234. Our books are also available through library jobbers and
regional distributors. For personal orders and catalogs, please write to
City Lights Books, 261 Columbus Avenue, San Francisco, CA 94133.

CITY LIGHTS BOOKS are edited by Lawrence Ferlinghetti and
Nancy J. Peters and published at the City Lights Bookstore, 261 Columbus
Avenue, San Francisco, CA 94133.

This book is for Sheppard,
compañero,
fellow traveler on the paths
of the Four Worlds . . .

CONTENTS

FOREWORD
For Diane

I've loved women all my life, this one especially—and for once I think I really know why. Williams, in a late poem, ends by saying, "The female principle of the world / is my appeal / in the extremity / to which I have come." We stretch out long on the earth, as men, thinking to take care of it, to give it specific form, to make manifest our experience in how we take hold. Yet there is no one there unless this *other* person of our reality take place too, with a generosity only possible in that act. Diane di Prima is fact of that "female principle" whereof Williams speaks—not simply, certainly not passively, but clearly, specifically, a woman as one might hope equally to be a man.

I am not speaking of roles, nor even of that political situation of persons she has so decisively herself entered at times. Nor of children and homes, though she has made both a deep and abiding pleasure in her own life and those related. It is some act of essential clarity I value—which in these initial occasions of her writing is already moving to declare itself: food, places, friends, nights, streets, dreams, the way. She is an adept and flexible provider of the real, which we eat daily or else we starve. She is kind but will not accept confusion. She is beautifully warm, but her nature balks at false responses. She is true.

Growing up in the fifties, you had to figure it out for yourself—which she did, and stayed open—as a woman, uninterested in any possibility of static investment or solution. Her search for human center is among the most moving I have witnessed—and she took her friends with her, though often it would have been simpler indeed to have gone alone. God bless her toughness and the deep gentleness of her hand!

—ROBERT CREELEY

THIRTEEN NIGHTMARES

NIGHTMARE 1

Well, I had gotten to a warmer place for starving and lived on beaches, and it seemed to me that everything would swing if I had some book or other. So I wrote my mother (found paper) and told her General Delivery and then I went back to beach and waited. Nights warm enough to sleep and fish ok and paper occasionally a poem, and then it seemed like time enough and I went to the post office.

A package I said a book my name is thus and they said identification please. And I looked in all pockets but a lucky wave had gotten the cards with my name.

Please I said, please please please. A book inside, Rimbaud, open and look for gods sake please.

Sorry they said why not go home they said and get your i.d.

Sure I said I'll ask that wave next time I see it but now give me package.

Sorry they said and put it on shelf
high
behind wire and screen. Rimbaud there and maybe food probably tucked around. Salami and cans of things food you know.

Please I said please well good day.

Good day they said.

NIGHTMARE 2

Having a cleaner house than usual I did the dishes. Gathering those long slime worms, dayold spaghetti, I dropped from the sink into the garbage them whereupon one slithered to the floor and lay there smirking.

Ugh I said but having a cleaner floor than usual I tried to pick it up, whereupon it nudged limply over and again smirked. After ten minutes of chase I with dirtier hands than usual gave up.

Oh well I said under the water faucet it will be hard as nails tonight the bastard and I'll pick it up stiff as a board.

Whereupon looking down again I saw a line of sleek roaches was marching the worm away and singing *Onward Christian Roaches.*

The din was unbearable and I remained horrored to the spot until a slightly larger roach, obviously leader, nudged me to see if I too could be carried off.

NIGHTMARE 3

Spent fascinated hours watching the uncool of a young moth doing herself in at the flame of my nonessential bohemian candle.

Which was ok, till she sideways gave up and clicked to crisp end of nothing curled with small smoke.

Which was ok till from across ceiling room leaped flew another, raced, and screaming "Dido" followed her.

NIGHTMARE 4

Many days hungry laid out on table dish raw chopped questionable meat probably edible, hope so, and went for matches.

Returned with frying pan somehow washed found on the table no meat, cat, no meat. Motherfucking bitch I said and flattened her with the frying pan squashed her bones practically dead and left her for tears. On bug-jumping bed I cried screamed and then cried to eventually recover and heel-toe to kitchen to see just to look and make sure.

On the table, still flat now stiff lay cat all dead not hungry now, but trails of drying sometime blood to floor and back told how she'd gone to get the now beside her meal (she thought) for me, a mouse she killed and died.

NIGHTMARE 5

Knock knock

Who is it I said

The man he said to turn your meter off.

Sorry I said but I'm in bed and things and come back later please.

I'll wait he said.

Do that I said and gave him 57 hours 40 minutes to give up. Went out then to hall jon, eagerly.

Hello he said

Hello I said

Sorry he said to turn your meter off. I gotta make a buck he said I gotta family.

I know I said its what they always say and go ahead. When you go home I'll saw the damn lock off.

That wont work now he said they gotta alloy. Spent 30 million dollars making it. Cant saw it thru no matter what he said.

OK I said go to it and go home. I'm going to the jon.

I did, he did, he left, I found a chair. And tried saw hammer chisel tried slipped bruised nails tried tried saw tried. Soup to cook.

Twelve hours later went to druggist. Sam I said I have a charge account for bennies give me some hydrofluoric acid.

Mac he said I dont know. Bennies is one thing Mac he said this acid jazz is something else.

Sam I said I gotta cook they locked the meter soup you know food you know.

OK Mac he said but take it easy.

Drip

Hole also in table, floor, maybe downstairs dont know but hole in lock too soup open great. Wow.

But ha no matches jokes on me the gas on and no matches let it go. Plenty of gas guess I wont eat.

4

NIGHTMARE 6

Get your cut throat off my knife.

NIGHTMARE 7

One day I forgot my sleeve and my heart pinned to my arm was burning a hole there.

Discovered in pocket fifty cents no more; on 42nd looked for a pleasant movie.

Until the most beautiful god he was I think up to me hood walked and smiled knowing everything and then knowing.

Are you busy he said and I laughed because no busy would be busier than seeing him and he knew it.

And he laughed knowing all and acknowledging simply yes that is so there is garish and hurt but not us.

And walked all three him and me and our hands between and he had a room where the ceiling danced for me danced all night.

Till morning awakened and yawning with dirty teeth he said well babe now how much do you get?

NIGHTMARE 8

Then I was standing in line unemployment green institution green room green people slow shuffle. Then to the man ahead said clerk-behind-desk, folding papers bored & sticking on seals

Here are your twenty reasons for living sir.

NIGHTMARE 9

Keep moving said the cop. The park closes at nine keep moving dammit. God damn things you think you own the park.

Not talking huh not going noplace? We'll see. Send you up for observation a week of shock will do you good I bet.

And he blew his whistle.

Whereupon white car pulled up,
white attendants
who set about their job without emotion.
It wasnt the first time theyd seen a catatonic tree.

NIGHTMARE 10

I saw it man, I read it in one of their god damned trade journals:

"Open season on people over 21 in dungarees or ancient sneakers,
men with lipstick,
women with crew cuts,
actors out of work,
poets of all descriptions. Bounty for heads ten dollars. Junkies and jazz musicians five dollars extra."

You can say I'm mad but that dont mean I'm crazy. Ask any cabdriver.

NIGHTMARE 11

I really must get a new vegetable brush. Everytime I forget and use it on my face the vegetables I scrub next day turn brown and kinda strange. . .

NIGHTMARE 12

I went to the clinic. I twisted my foot I said.

Whats your name they said and age and how much do you make and whos your family dentist.

I told them and they told me to wait and I waited and they said come inside and I did.

Open your eye said the doctor you have something in it.

I hurt my foot I said.

Open your eye he said and I did and he took out the eyeball and washed it in a basin.

There he said and put it back that feels better doesnt it.

I guess so I said. Its all black I dont know. I hurt my foot I said.

Would you mind blinking he said one of your eyelashes is loose.

I think I said theres something the matter with my foot.

Oh he said. Perhaps you're right. I'll cut it off.

NIGHTMARE 13

It hurts to be murdered.

MORE OR LESS LOVE POEMS

*
they all say
you're lovely
but everytime I look
the sun
(or something else)
gets in my eyes

*
Yeah that was
once in a lifetime
baby

you gotta be clean and
with new shoes
to love like I loved you.

I think it won't happen again.

*
damn you
lovely
you come and go
like rivers
which makes it hard
on rocks

*

In case you put me down I put you down
already, doll
I know the games you play

In case you put me down I got it figured
how there are better mouths than yours
more swinging bodies
wilder scenes than this.

In case you put me down it won't help much.

*

In your arms baby
I don't feel no
spring in winter
but I guess I can do
without
galoshes.

In your arms baby
I don't hear no
angels sing
but maybe I forget
to turn on
the phonograph.

*

your tongue
explodes
like jailbreaks
in my head

*
No aperture of your body I do not know
no way into your gut I have not studied

so now
we pause for this finesse
silk at your temples
and
in the hollow of your neck
a tongue
goes gently

*
I hope
you go thru hell
tonight
beloved.
I hope
you choke to death
on lumps of stars
and by your bed a window
with frost
and moon on frost and
you want to scream
and can't
because
your woman is (I hope)
right there
asleep.

Baby I hope you never shut your eyes
so two of us
can pick up on
this dawn.

*
you are not quite
the air I breathe
thank god

so go.

*
you bet your life
next bedtime
I'll get even

I'll call your name wrong
and you'll think
it happened
accidental

*
the word you whispered
turned your hair
to snakes
and that star
your face
went nearly out

*

long gone that light behind you
gone
that light
that made the edges of your shoulders live
and kept your face a secret

*

for you
i would no longer pick
my so-pickable nose
or bite my delicious nails

for you i would fix my teeth
and buy a mattress

for you
i'd kill my favorite roach
that lives in the woodwork
by the drawing table

*

shuddering the dark
rocks us both in her arms
from her tongue red flowers spring
from between her thighs
the white gull flies, he moans, we spill aside
his highboned chest cuts forward
finds its rhythm
he pins with amorous wing the struggling
moon

12

*

So much of space between us two
We kiss the planets when we kiss
No closeness ever shuts this out
So much of space between us two

We kiss the planets when we kiss
And all the ether knows your hand
And dust from Saturn foils my tongue
So much black light caresses us

No closeness ever shuts this out
But mouth from shoulder, thigh from thigh
Explosive air unwinds our love
So distance holds, so love is safe

REQUIEM

I think
you'll find
a coffin
not so good
Baby-O.
They strap you in
pretty tight

I hear
it's cold
and worms and things
are there for selfish reasons

I think
you'll want
to turn
onto your side
your hair
won't like
to stay in place
forever
and your hands
won't like it
crossed
like that

I think
your lips
won't like it
by themselves

THREE LAMENTS

1
Alas
I believe
I might have become
a great writer
but
the chairs
in the library
were too hard

2
I have
the upper hand
but if I keep it
I'll lose the circulation
in one arm

3
So here I am the coolest in New York
what dont swing I dont push.

In some Elysian field
by a big tree
I chew my pride
like cud.

MINOR ARCANA

Body
whose flesh
has crossed my will?
Which night
common or blest
shapes now
to walk the earth?

Body
whose hands
broke ground
for that thrusting head?
in the eyes
budding to sight
who will I read?

Body
secret in you
sprang this cry of flesh

Now tell the tale

SONG FOR BABY-O, UNBORN

Sweetheart
when you break thru
you'll find
a poet here
not quite what one would choose.

I won't promise
you'll never go hungry
or that you won't be sad
on this gutted
breaking
globe

but I can show you
baby
enough to love
to break your heart
forever

THE WINDOW

you are my bread
and the hairline
noise
of my bones
you are almost
the sea

you are not stone
or molten sound
I think
you have no hands

this kind of bird flies backward
and this love
breaks on a windowpane
where no light talks

this is not time
for crossing tongues
(the sand here
never shifts)

I think
tomorrow
turned you with his toe
and you will
shine
and shine
unspent and underground

SHORT NOTE ON THE SPARSENESS
OF THE LANGUAGE

wow man I said
when you tipped my chin and fed
on headlong spit my tongue's libation fluid

and wow I said when we hit the mattressrags
and wow was the dawn: we boiled the coffeegrounds
in an unkempt pot

wow man I said the day you put me down
(only the tone was different)
wow man oh wow   I took my comb
and my two books and cut and that was that

THE PRACTICE OF MAGICAL EVOCATION

The female is fertile, and discipline
(contra naturam) only
                    confuses her
                              —Gary Snyder

i am a woman and my poems
are woman's: easy to say
this.   the female is ductile
and
        (stroke after stroke)
built for masochistic
calm.   The deadened nerve
is part of it:
awakened sex, dead retina
fish eyes;   at hair's root
minimal feeling

and pelvic architecture functional
assailed inside & out
(bring forth)   the cunt gets wide
and relatively sloppy
bring forth men children only
                              female
                              is
                              ductile

woman, a veil thru which the fingering Will
twice torn
twice torn
              inside & out
the flow
what rhythm add to stillness
what applause?

FOR ZELLA, PAINTING

1
what are you.
thinking.
at night/these nights/night
when
(unsleeping)
the red.
the hills
where you walk.

and who could tolerate that sky.

2
what blue is that
your eyes
your lumpy shirt

while you.
stand.
slumping in dawn light
(same blue)

and from your hands the cadmiums run, shouting.

POETICS

I have deserted my post, I cdnt hold it
rearguard/to preserve the language/lucidity:
let the language fend for itself.
it turned over god knows enough carts in the city streets
its barricades are my nightmares

preserve the language!—there are
                enough fascists &
                enough socialists
on both sides
so that no one will lose this war

the language shall be my element, I plunge in
I suspect that I cannot drown
like a fat brat catfish, smug
                a hoodlum fish
I move more & more gracefully
                breathe it in,
success written on my mug till the fishpolice
corner me in the coral & I die

VECTOR

for Jean Cocteau

I.
this: to X plode
the love affair with space.
that the void penetrate
        make talons
        make like fangs
        slip in

mist is an incarnation much desired
the modeling of light

if I cd hold a skirt in one hand, wait
while people (male) opened doors
never dream
of the women's jon or dancing chicks
putting on tights
this is irrelevant, the stars
are always blackest on the other side of the void
if I cd get hot pants for you, not just
the affable desirings of warmth
        how we are friends!
not to pick up dropped lipstick
                open doors
the flip side of the coin

how it is an ankle over a spike heel
& the turn & curve of a junkie's cheek & nose
are aesthetically equal
                        chill
and quite beyond me
        fumbling from pregnancy to space
on my way to an ultimate scattering of atoms

selfconscious, yes
to BE THOUGHT WELL OF
               &
to DO AS PLEASE
               two hangups
I tapdance, looking over my shoulder
sit in the audience w/greasepaint on
examine separately the hundred petals
                 of flowers sent
counting them at night
in a dark room
       my miser's glee
       devising new crevices always.

I sleep on my stomach, chin
                digging into the pillow
is that what you want to know?

to outsmart space
       to come on colder
than the void
       that's one way—
still enuf & you hit 0
      (zero)
      [absolute]
   turn up yr toes, there!
   a little more white to the eyes!
ol Rigor
        (father) Mortis
        cut me in.

to outstrip space go halfway out to meet it
or to sit, bald & shiny, while a drop
of ink   from the ordained hand
              fell, making pictures
you a constellation
          & all that cold air
          inbetween yr eyes

II.
I'm in headlong flight from something I will meet
the hand in my back just below the shoulder blades
Eumenides?
        the stars
        with streaming hair
        scream laugh awake
my feet havent touched the ground in years
a gentle wobbling motion
        side to side

and the light focuses
        is gently led
        thru prisms, lenses
comes at last to point
        & burns
        the paper smokes
all space is smoking & my hair streams back

light flat like on snow
        coming head on
        hits
like an open hand on the back of the neck
cut steps in ice, all you get is hit more times
cut steps   the hand is gold
        light streams out from it
        or seems to
the secret is:
        LIGHT NEVER STREAMS OUT
only back.
        I always wear a raincoat
hands in the pockets pull back
        (it's never buttoned)
and I walk forward out of it
        unembarrassed

THE JUNGLE
for Roi

1
time & time again the laughter after the footsteps
in the snow, the moths walk stiffly
dont palm off yr deathshead on me, man,
or yr horse with the broken leg
        on stilts
        always on stilts
hair brushing the stars, the hair ends cracking

and this is NY   nothing but sleet & foghorns
we'd have to answer the door again someday you know:
the sleet, kissing the window like a goldfish
like a sick goldfish, a goldfish gone to seed;
300 watts in my ceiling, 3 eyes regard me:
the claw lowered behind me on a web.
where's the cellar where you never wet yr feet?
        whose sound is it?

dont come in no cravat to this falling door
two deathblows it had
I shall stop shaking someday
        the beasts cry out:
lushpadded, making it, the growth slimy
they walk, paths never crossing, like dancers
their tails erect, or swishing, or they droop
but their eyes
        the rain falls on the leaves
        the leaves
fall; tenderfooted they walk, tendergrowling, all of love
in the deathspring

2

tomatoes on the vine,
            but that green fruit
juggled too soon,
            it rots before it ripes
its sweet all in its seed
                        its gay tomorrows.
who says we shall not die, the sleet counts off
that Mr. Goldberg has the cheapest tombstones
on Rivington, but Schultz, he does the carving
makes you cry.
I shall put on my seven league boots
and go out picking daisies.
Bullshit.
I shall sit in a freezing pad
while my door gets deathblows.
            how my window's bruised
blue fleshmarks on the glass.
the wind ignores me, glances off my cunt
            my knuckles
            & the corners of my mouth.
the wind is pink, it makes the snow obscene.

3

tomorrow the fire went out, under the small porch, the snail
regarded the matter, retreated,
            backing into an asymmetrical web
a foot came thru the ceiling, someone turned the knob
on the cancerous door.
I will let you lay yr hand on my head again
but in another fashion.
            Rape of the spirit,
that was
& this a holiday for pears
            if only banners streamed
in different directions
            if only a single face
were turned away. . .

4

to drop the fucking thing & watch it burn
if it were in my hands, the atomic war wd be past history.
how cosmic chill
passes from one to other as we kiss.
I walk with every beast that walks in me
more catfooted than they
but at the kill, exultant, all of wind
is nothing to this.
                    It's a losing game.
I walk with every beast that walks
            to take the dragon
thru the city gates
            neck with the cyclops,
etc.
            Eumenides, if one face turns
away
            and the wind, which we must
swallow, whatever we will.

5

that the sea shd only pay us a flying visit
that the flowers scattered on it do not change
the least of its plans.
my hands are in the wind's mouth, I am led
my eyes are blank,
            nothing is in my hands.
the wall in front of me cuts off sound & sight
my head is chained
nothing is in my hands.
no vines grow on the wall, from time to time
the rain
brings down a rumor of the sky.

that we have floated together away from the fire
that the castle has turned to cardboard, that the air
               will not go near us.
somewhere the wind plays only on the grass
dark and light the turning in the air

that the block of ice which binds us
                              binds us both.

THE PARTY

1

war is our carnival
        the scent of it
high in our nostrils
        like snow
        like coke
the tambourines, the eternal tight-rope walk
dogs bark at the river's edge
madonna lilies lurking in the corners

the evil fucking symmetry of it
stars have no symmetry, nor my hair let down
nor us, when we're making it,
                like really making it
ghosts are not formal, tho they stand in doorways.
give me your hand, goddammit
GIVE ME YOUR HAND

the world cd end, or I cd slip off the edge
& you not know, the snow is so deep
like, where are you now, not here, and the air is falling
airstorm we're having, baby, not wind but air
I need another cloak
        yr fingertips
on my cheek
I NEED TO BE LOOKED AT
        be seen
& not twice a week
I'm not a Brancusi bird
                not self-sufficient

2
yr hand
peeling an orange
the green plant growing
        in the light
        in the window
the curtains slightly dirty
cabs move outside, their
            lights (lanterns
tracing out the mist.
        what violence do we wait for?
at the table
        I cut a melon
        symmetrically in thirds
set one aside.

you are dressed in something you wd never wear
it is loose & ragged & very beautiful
a child
        plays naked on the floor
        the floor is clean
fruit trees are in the garden
I am happy

3

we turn the corner, go another way
cobbles/the lofts, the silent loading platforms
bums make a bonfire
                    I hold out my hand
but yrs are covered w/rings
                    I have a bundle
you stop at a door
                    I do not trust it
the bell
        has another name.
I put the bundle down, and walk away
my skirt swings,
                    my high heels
a trolley clangs

        do you know what I'm trying to say
that we shall never have a bowl of goldfish
on a low table, where the sun comes in
this is the whole damned void, the chill,
                    my way
to say goodbye

THE YEOMAN OF THE GUARD

the simplicity of it, you said, a different universe
what we were led to expect
    drinking ale from blue glass in the dark
    the couch dark, too

grapes grew in clusters from the ceiling, yet
somehow the satyrs, if that's what they were,
    in the corners,
the satyrs had a decadent air
    bald & lined like old fags
lurking in dull bars
if any beasts walked they were deadly

tomorrow, I said, I shall polish the floor,
    make curtains
tomorrow I shall come to the door w/my hair down
the mistress *par excellence*
    & offer you brandy

you shall brush my hair
    like Charles Boyer in a movie
& I (like Hedy Lamarr) shall tilt back my head
& suddenly smile

LORD JIM

forcing it thru yr teeth like the red syrup
that keeps us from coughing at night
I have begun to walk toward it,
                          it is very beautiful
                          I shall walk toward it
all my flesh
protesting, do you see, the sun makes light
by exploding, by eating away

I am not afraid.   That is a lie
                          & it is another lie
to say I will stay.

I SHALL WALK TOWARD IT
                          the green ice flickers & leaps
the summer shall send down hail
I want very little:

that you shd make light/make love
                          consent
to be corroded, blind, the hissing steam
rising at once from both of us

In the summer the empty lot, at the end of the sidewalk
is covered w/matted grasses, dry, the flickering
backs of beetles. . .

thru the uncertainty, the poise
                of listening.
the drop of ink falls. It lands. It makes a shape.
SOMEONE HAS CRIED OUT TO ME, HAS ASKED FOR LIFE
something has stirred in there, behind the trees.
I am afraid of the shapes I must make on the stage
all the air I must cut thru.

I am afraid of yr face, yr silence, the laugh
w/which you carry it off.
I want to tell you we'll die
                why stand for it
why take what's offered, why not walk toward
the green & flickering sea that comes to meet us

THE BEACH

where I ship out from, the tides
                        give no indication
washing dead flowers, under the rocks
at my back; the houses flat & implacable
painted green. It peels. The walls are damp.

The chill at the railroad station in the mornings
always the dawn light & wind,
                        our collars turned up
the suitcases broken, a gesture. Almost empty.
Ourselves the pitiful grey of no baths, no sleep
the grey we rub off the sheets
in the green houses. Did we lock the door
the sea is gold in the dawn light, the rocks
silhouetted against it.

how many years will you amble along the shore
hands in yr pockets, whistling the same old tune?
living on softshell crabs, the seafloor hard
under yr clean bare feet.
Just as I caught the train I think I saw you
shuffling to the horizon to stamp it flat

that was before the picnic basket fell open
& my choice, my monster lobster walked back
home

BLACKOUT

machinery has no part in it, what comes apart
here, in the air, makes no claim,
CAN NOT BE FIXED
the trees, dropping caterpillars
on our heads, which are upright w/difficulty.

Children pull up the grasses, they spew out
a chorus of smells.   Your hands
                have aged this week
Just yr hands.   These things
                begin slowly.
My face has just tilted down, the weight of eyeballs
the grass smell, the smell of child spit, yr
hands. When I saw them, on my shoulder,
a different person.
                and then the face
pressed to the window, the two hands
one on each side of it—

yr real hands out there, the fingertips pale
from pressing the glass.

Make more of diamonds.
       Not every day
do you find in the grass
       jewels, colored eggs
        the bones of chickens.
Excitement.
Try laughter.
Or a good, surprised, shout.
       Manlike.
The kind of yell that's heard in Alaska.

Like velvet, like powdered snow, the skin on yr stomach
the skin on yr back. I fold my hands.
Under my cheek.
                    and take it all.
          What is offered & what is not.
Your laugh. Your hands at the window, wanting in.

MONTEZUMA

to give it away, give it up, before they take it from us.
not to go down fighting.

the hard part comes later
to see the women taken, the young men maimed
the city
no city is built twice
the long wall down at Athens, the olive trees
                   five hundred years of tillage
burning. "not these but men"
i.e., mourn
        not these

and yet no city is ever built again

NUMBERS RACKET

when you take no for an answer
will you look any different
will you get pale
behind your glasses will you
go backward with that
funny step
will you straighten your jacket

I mean are you taking it.
now, taking no
for an answer.

BABYLONIA

the star rises over the stone gates.
a period of silence, which will be followed by rain.
a red flower in the greys, in the wet field
the red flower opens,
            a cry, a bitter cry.

anecdote of the child, in the ancestral basket
about its neck a string of water lilies
the hut fallen to pieces, wood rotted, flaking off
the sound of breathing, an old woman cooking potatoes
a chandelier creaks from the rotted ceiling
the child holds up his fist, and smiles.
the dog in the corner stirs.

a string of water lilies; in a corner
a heap of rubies, the old woman
bent at the fire.

creation of parsley

the young man, who was green
stept out of the river.
wherever he walked, herbs grew
and they smelled sweet.
the young man walked back
into the river.
he sank like a stone.

I CHING

for Cecil Taylor

                    :mountain & lake
the breakup
                of configurations.
all the persian rugs in the world
                are doing a dance,
or conversely smoke.

outside my window the hoods are shouting
                      about Ty Cobb
on Friday nite it was girls
                & they were drunk.
But the white car stays the same
                that they lean against.

COSCIA'S: NOVEMBER 1963

(Letter to John Wieners)

I expect a certain amount of
respect
yes I do
as do you
(don't like to be called "girlie")
a certain amount of deference
stopping to listen
when I pronounce
an opinion.
Arrogance, as they have it, in one so young
one young enough to indulge in
arrogance

The greatcoats stride
and pride
drips off of me. With my braids uncombed
unsightly
so I be.
And you? You prance in rags
in Boston rags
thru department stores you dance
you prance
on top of the Charles
not breaking grammar's rules
nor respecting them,
uncouth & incomplete
definitive

Or you stop at a counter maybe
costume jewelry
sparkles before you.
Your long, definéd, filthy
highclass fingers
close over it.
                    another brooch
nestles beneath your dirty handkerchief.
What your hands don't know of aristocracy
ain't nobody now remembers those nuances

It is going to snow,
Toys are frozen to the roof
They are loading meat in foul smelling trucks
on 6th Street. I have eaten my eggs.
Dogs look like wolves, the city closes in
the sky, the winter and the wettening air.
What more tiara now, for you or I?

ON SITTING DOWN TO WRITE,
I DECIDE INSTEAD TO GO TO
FRED HERKO'S CONCERT

As water, silk
the quiver of fish
or the long cry of goose
            or some such bird
            I never heard
your orange tie
a sock in the eye
            as Duncan
            might forcibly note
are you sitting under the irregular drums
of Brooklyn Joe Jones
(in a loft which I know to be dirty
& probably cold)
or have you scurried already
                hurried already
uptown
on a Third Avenue Bus
toward smelly movies & crabs I'll never get
and you all perfumed too
as if they'd notice

O the dark caves of obligation
into which I must creep
            (alack)
like downstairs & into a coat
            O all that wind
Even Lord & Taylor don't quite keep out
that wind

and that petulant vacuum
I am aware of it
sucking me into Bond Street
into that loft
      dank
      rank
I draw a blank
at the very thought

          Hello
I came here
      after all

RONDEAU FOR THE YULE

I got away with it all summer will
I get away with it all fall
& more importantly winter.
Infinitesimal yearnings, the romantic
or western concept of love
(not Traherne's)
familiar concept.

It fills
the cup in me with thorns
I am cruel to the children.
That is,
You stride up the street & I
get on a bus.
We got away with it for the past three years.

Another escaping & you are not so dumb
That you didn't see that in it.
There are Xmas decorations in the windows.
Four Christmases ago, or the summer before
and mostly ephemeral.
The seasons roll over it,
flattening it out.
Still, a flicker of interest: what a funny hat
You're wearing.

Rejoice!
Architectonic bells
Motets of pain.
Anger, or is it just the wind is cold?

Exultate!
a thin grey cry
that the eagles carry between
my bus & your walking;

O beautiful city
juggling us both in its hands
playing jacks with us like an unskillful girl
O winter closing down on our separate shells

ODE TO ELEGANCE

from *The Calculus of Variation*

AND PRAISE THE GRACE, the elegance of body. Your hands,
flesh of my children, thin giraffes
raising themselves in the sun on distant plains
The elegance of mantis and of beetle
The clear precisions of the shooting stars
colors of water
sounds on the city air
directio voluntatis, the clear will
shining like rubies through the lucid eyes
"the city of Dioce"
long eyes of cats in the grass

the slender elegance of scorpions
lovers of death
flash of the hunting knife
the thin high noise in the air
the breath of Kali
precision of the fingernail on flesh
pastels of Beardsley
pain of a century

that the skin should lie so elegantly on the air
that the black night should penetrate so gently
that treason should shine like stars
the clarity
of dawn, of murder, of the running tide

the subtle stuff of slime, the river mosses
with light inwoven
the elegance of the skull
the phosphorescence of the ending body
exposed to earth to air water or fire
will o'the wisp, a marsh light, star to star
the holy mother of the cremation ground

let us now praise all fleshly consummations
(the elegance of sweat)
initiation
into the burning loneliness of this place
desert of salt
immense intoxication
in this white light
under this rush of wind
all things teem forth like dust motes in the air

that all things send forth love, inanimate
that all these loves have mingled in the air
and set up a great clangor
in the nodes
heart of this sound, this deadly spirit love
a cosmos comes to birth

let the pure pain tear your throat till you spit blood
cry out! rejoice!
that which must come to birth
even the goddessmother cannot dream of

we climb from rung to rung, a circular
undeviating golden, perfect ladder
of ages, long forgotten, to be told
over and over, like a string of prayerbeads

"the ferris wheel has started up again"

I GET MY PERIOD, SEPTEMBER 1964

How can I forgive you this blood?
Which was not to flow again, but to cling joyously to my womb
To grow, and become a son?

When I turn to you in the night, you sigh, and turn over
When I turn to you in the afternoon, on our bed,
Where you lie reading, you put me off, saying only
It is hot, you are tired.

You picket, you talk of violence, *you draw blood*
But only from me, unseeded & hungry blood
Which meant to be something else.

FOR THE DEAD LECTURER

We must convince the living
that the dead
cannot sing.
                    —LeRoi Jones

THE DEAD CAN SING
and do
muttering thru beards of old vanilla
malteds, soft shoe
loving, the tin noises of cheap refrigerators.
I have heard you creaking
over the roof at night to steal my books
coming in thru the telephone wires
just when my head
was empty
When Milarepa & other Tantric wisdom
was clambering thru my skull
suddenly again your bumpy face
in my arms
the rags of your winter clothes
hitting my broken windows
(who else would have stolen the Poems of
John Skelton
of Tu Fu
or Thomas Traherne
Who else left that aroma
of pot & sweat, tobacco smoke & beer
((tears))
on my sofa?)

You dead sing now, thru your eyes,
they push up jade trees
they start
out of the skull of your daughter
asleep in my arms
and why not talk of these things
are we less faithful than bisons
or giraffes?

I'll tangle my crest with yours, like scorpions
and kill you for love
I'll kill you yet
so your song can fill my life.

FIRST SNOW, KERHONKSON

for Alan

This, then, is the gift the world has given me
(you have given me)
softly the snow
cupped in hollows
lying on the surface of the pond
matching my long white candles
which stand at the window
which will burn at dusk while the snow
fills up our valley
this hollow
no friend will wander down
no one arriving brown from Mexico
from the sunfields of California, bearing pot
they are scattered now, dead or silent
or blasted to madness
by the howling brightness of our once common vision
and this gift of yours—
white silence filling the contours of my life.

THE BUS RIDE

I thought at first it was from the shore of Sicily you had taken me
Coming out of some feudal hall on the Baltic Sea
But the memory is older:

Was it the shore of Crete you plundered
In your Tartar coat, and that strange leather hat?

I know that you took me north and away from the sea
—As I ride now in this bus—that I mourned a little
for my painted cloth and fine enameled chests

Did you take me from China, out of India
to the sweep of the Gobi desert, tents heavy with plunder
where I longed for my books and the sound of my own tongue,
the saris with gold inwoven—you were brave
and kind to me, taller than any man
of my own race—I slowly learned to love you
as I am learning now:

    our Tartar son
    plays in Kerhonkson in his chilly room
    in these northern mountains where you have taken me

the silk screens covered with calligraphy
poems of the old time I set up about me
came down in that desert wind. . .

coming upon you in morning meditation
I find in your eyes the light of the first man
greeting the winter sun at the edge of the world.

BUDDHIST NEW YEAR SONG

I saw you in green velvet, wide full sleeves
seated in front of a fireplace, our house
made somehow more gracious, and you said
"There are stars in your hair"—it was truth I
brought down with me

to this sullen and dingy place that we must make golden
make precious and mythical somehow, it is our nature,
and it is truth, that we came here, I told you,
from other planets
where we were lords, we were sent here,
for some purpose

the golden mask I had seen before, that fitted
so beautifully over your face, did not return
nor did that face of a bull you had acquired
amid northern peoples, nomads, the Gobi desert

I did not see those tents again, nor the wagons
infinitely slow on the infinitely windy plains,
so cold, every star in the sky was a different color
the sky itself a tangled tapestry, glowing
but almost, I could see the planet from which we had come

I could not remember (then) what our purpose was
but remembered the name Mahakala, in the dawn

in the dawn confronted Shiva, the cold light
revealed the "mindborn" worlds, as simply that,
I watched them propagated, flowing out,
or, more simply, one mirror reflecting another.
then broke the mirrors, you were no longer in sight
nor any purpose, stared at this new blackness
the mindborn worlds fled, and the mind turned off:

a madness, or a beginning?

ODE TO KEATS

1

Had you lived longer than your 26 years
You, too, wd have come up against it like a wall—
That the Beauty you saw was bought
At too great a price
Even in those days:
The weavers, Ireland, the misery in dark streets
The earth torn up
The rich loam thrown aside
Shacks mushrooming everywhere to house
The children of the poor.

Of whom I am one.
Of whom you are one.

Are we, indeed, welcome at Millbrook
In the great estate houses
Their moldings crumble, woodpanels scratched
By pencils & hairpins in the hands of the infants of the poor
Are we, indeed, welcome to the fruits of the earth

Shreds, patches of velvet & satin, shards of old glass, the opulence
Remnants of a broken culture, you too, even then
Wd have seen it, had you lived longer.

And wd you shout, as some of us shout now, "Clear!
Clear the earth of the clutter of foul-smelling shacks
Clear the great old houses of the barbarian hordes
Who sleep on mattresses on all their floors
Who are even now burning high-backed Spanish chairs
In the great fireplaces—
Who clutter the beach so the face of the sea can no longer be seen. . ."

You, telling your beads on primroses, hanging up Shakespeare
On the Isle of Wight, you, the footman's son—
Did you know who would follow us in when we opened the door
To step into opulence, to dream among these curtains?
And are we accountable? And to whom?

2   The Dream

Hedged about as we are with prayers
And with taboos
Yet the heart of the magic circle is covered with grey linoleum
Over my head fly demons of the past
    Roi   Lori   Jimmy, they pass
With a whooshing sound
The only ghost who stands on the ground
   (who stands his ground)
Is Freddie—
I rise a few inches above the circle, and turn somersaults
I want to go shopping, but all I see is my reflection
I look tired and sad. I wear red. I am looking for love.
On the sidewalk are lying the sick and the hungry:
I hear "Spencer's *Faerie Queene* cost them all their lives."
And Spencer? I ask, "What did his life buy?"
Through the door is the way out, Alan stands in the doorway
In an attitude of leaving, his head is turned
As if to say goodbye, but he's standing still.

Hedged about with primroses
         with promises
The magic words we said when we were praying
Have formed a mist about us. . .

3   *Note to Roi*

I wonder often what it is that you are doing—
How much of it *is* pride, or ambition
As we so easily say.
I remember the message I gave Freddie for you
That I would see you again at the end of this
(Meaning my marriage and yours)
Not dreaming how far that would take us:
Freddie dead—
You living in Harlem, where you'll surely be killed
Gunned down, like Malcolm X, in some hotel
Or haberdasher's shop—some bleak room or street
Without my having told you you were my love
Among the adventures & common sense of my life.

4

Will you come to visit me, Keats, in this house, like you used to?
Bringing a blanket to put across your knees—
Stand leaning on the cupboard with typing paper
Or sit on the trunk of cloth in my chilly bedroom?
It's a place without grace or luxury, a backwater
Where, perhaps, the "life of the mind" can flourish.
I hardly see you here—I hope you will come.
I am entering the heart of loneliness
And I remember dimly the house you came to
When I was younger, and poetry was a wall
To be scaled, by hook or crook
Was a house of mean proportions, rather like this
With roses on the linoleum in my bedroom

The visions begin on the pale green wall of my study
They burn in the darkness—
I SHALL MELT INTO THEM.

IN MEMORY OF MY FIRST CHAPATIS

If we had dope for an excuse, or love,
something bumpier, with ups and downs
(like the chapatis, puffing & going stiff—
I probably overcooked them) to account for
your incessant displeasures.

You stalk around the house, brandishing T-squares
you dream of drowning the children
you tell me nine days of the week that you are leaving
but you're still here. I can tell by the lump in my stomach
my unreasonable desire to sleep all the time

so as not to hear you starting the Volkswagen Bus
as if it were a Mercedes, zooming out of the driveway

The women of the rest of the world have so much to teach me!
Them in their saris so cool, kneading chapatis
or tortillas, depending on where, kneeling by their fires
or by their hibachis, or standing by their wood stoves
the women of the rest of the world plait their hair as I do
but they have more patience, they have put up a screen

behind which they only dimly discern their menfolk
bursting the air with perennial desperations.

BIOLOGY LESSON

It's sinister how everything comes alive
in the summer: on my light-table now,
> one small flea-like creature, doing backwards jumps
> one flat thing, looking rather like a date-pit
> with legs; one fly(?) with strip-ed wings

downstairs the compost garbage grows pink mold
every night, over whatever I threw away
the day before: weird smell, too; if I leave the cornmeal open
a field mouse, or equally tiny creature leaves droppings
on its top, after eating a gigantic meal

something lives in the wall of my bedroom, is never home
except on rare occasions (rainy nights)
the whole place practically crawls
> the green moist chilly warmth yin air
> busy as hell, the whole thing coming together
all over the place

they were dead wrong about no spontaneous
generation

PRAJAPATI

O Lord of Beasts
Herder of stars across the heavens
Hill god
Rudra
Who walks at dusk
We are all your beasts, who walk on these blue hills
Drawn by the sound of your bells
We hear your dance
Lord of the mountain
Young man with matted hair
There, in your bracelets—
Look, he raises his foot, the universe
Dissolves. He raises his hand
His hand says, have no fear.
Rush to see this, you maidens and young men
The king of the mountain is dancing
Draw closer
Look in his eyes

POEM IN PRAISE OF MY HUSBAND (Taos)

I suppose it hasn't been easy living with me either,
with my piques, and ups and downs, my need for privacy
leo pride and weeping in bed when you're trying to sleep
and you, interrupting me in the middle of a thousand poems
did I call the insurance people? the time you stopped a poem
in the middle of our drive over the nebraska hills and
into colorado, odetta singing, the whole world singing in me
the triumph of our revolution in the air
me about to get that down, and you
you saying something about the carburetor
so that it all went away

but we cling to each other
as if each thought the other was the raft
and he adrift alone, as in this mud house
not big enough, the walls dusting down around us, a fine dust rain
counteracting the good, high air, and stuffing our nostrils
we hang our pictures of the several worlds:
new york collage, and san francisco posters,
set out our japanese dishes, chinese knives
hammer small indian marriage cloths into the adobe
we stumble thru silence into each other's gut

blundering thru from one wrong place to the next
like kids who snuck out to play on a boat at night
and the boat slipped from its moorings, and they look at the stars
about which they know nothing, to find out
where they are going

NOVEMBER

for John Braden

if there's one pain that I can't bear
it's this pain of early parting
for our first sorrow had ended
and our first joy was just starting
and the loss that filled our bed, love
was the loss of children meeting
and the joy that filled our house
had come to stay
if you hear me where you're wandering
then know I send you greeting
and if you'll turn back
I'll wait another day

but the tall grass where you wander
holds no path back to my door
and the whisper of your hair upon the wind
for the past three days has told me
I'll be seeing you no more
and the fancy we called love has made an end

for the giant of the mountain
waits your footstep on his land
and the princess of the fountain
teaches more than I had planned
there's a skeleton on fire
that will lead you by the hand
to the caves beyond the grasses
rising from the leaden sand
where jewels shine in the dark
and ivory boats embark
for Avalon
from which there's no returning. . .

I know, like a living statue
you move with marble feet
through the towns that dot the grasses on your way
and you hide in cloak of iron
from the children on the street
and you tell yourself your flesh will warm someday

but the giant of the mountain
waits your footstep on his land
and the princess of the fountain
teaches more than I had planned
and the tall grass where you wander
holds no path back to my door
and the whisper of your hair upon the wind
for the past three days has told me
I'll be seeing you no more
and the fancy we called love has made an end

ZERO

for Lee Fitzgerald

a blessing on your velvet shoes
and on your hair so free
and may the wind that bore you here
soon take you away from me

for you are the Fool, the holy man
who wanders ceaselessly
and the star you follow does not stop
for my door and my company

a blessing on your coat so green
all worked with magic signs
and on the light in your bright eyes
unlike the light in mine

for joy is calling from the wind
and the white sun beats down
and at the end of your long, bright path
Puck polishes your crown

he holds it out on the Ace of Swords
no easy gift gives he
and the Fool becomes the Hanged Man
for that bright company

so may your wallet e'er be full
with goodly bread and meat
and the white dog who follows you
dance lightly at your feet

and may you mate with faerie girls
all in their robes of white
your long hands pluck anemones
late in the purple night

you shall drink wine from the jewelled Cup
and be drunk eternally
and wash your face in the silver foam
thrown by the pale grey sea

and the crown you gather shall not fade
though my tears will drop like leaves
and the wine you drink shall keep you warm
while all the northland grieves

for you are the Fool, and the Hanged Man
whose light shines endlessly
and that cruel wind that bore you here
bears you on eternally

CHRONOLOGY

I loved you in October
when you hid behind your hair
and rode your shadow
in the corners of the house

and in November you invaded
filling the air
above my bed with dreams
cries for some kind of help
on my inner ear

in December I held your hands
one afternoon; the light failed
it came back on
in a dawn on the Scottish coast
you singing us ashore

now it is January, you are fading
into your double
jewels on his cape, your shadow on the snow,
you slide away on wind, the crystal air
carries your new songs in snatches thru the windows
of our sad, high, pretty rooms

APRIL FOOL BIRTHDAY POEM
FOR GRANDPA

Today is your
birthday and I have tried
writing these things before,
but now
in the gathering madness, I want to
thank you
for telling me what to expect
for pulling
no punches, back there in that scrubbed Bronx parlor
thank you
for honestly weeping in time to
innumerable heartbreaking
italian operas for
pulling my hair when I
pulled the leaves off the trees so I'd
know how it feels, we are
involved in it now, revolution, up to our
knees and the tide is rising, I embrace
strangers on the street, filled with their love and
mine, the love you told us had to come or we
die, told them all in that Bronx park, me listening in
spring Bronx dusk, breathing stars, so glorious
to me your white hair, your height your fierce
blue eyes, rare among italians, I stood
a ways off, looking up at you, my grandpa
people listened to, I stand
a ways off listening as I pour out soup
young men with light in their faces
at my table, talking love, talking revolution
which is love, spelled backwards, how
you would love us all, would thunder your anarchist wisdom

at us, would thunder Dante, and Giordano Bruno, orderly men
bent to your ends, well I want you to know
we do it for you, and your ilk, for Carlo Tresca,
for Sacco and Vanzetti, without knowing
it, or thinking about it, as we do it for Aubrey Beardsley
Oscar Wilde (all street lights
shall be purple), do it
for Trotsky and Shelley and big/dumb
Kropotkin
Eisenstein's Strike people, Jean Cocteau's ennui, we do it for
the stars over the Bronx
that they may look on earth
and not be ashamed.

SEATTLE SONG

for Peter Coyote

Stray cat, climbing in my window
Stray cat, creeping up the stair
Stray cat, sliding thru the hallway
Cat, I wonder if you are there
Cat, I wonder if you are there

Stray cat, eating in my kitchen
Stray cat, sleeping in my bed
It's been a month since I have seen you
Cat, I wonder if you are dead
Cat, I wonder you alive or dead

You came crying in the hallway
Let you in and I stroked your hair
Fed you good and I let you ramble
Cause I was happy that you was there
I so happy that you was there

One day you started in to wander
Down the fire-escape and into the night
I leaned out my kitchen window
And watched you till you were out of sight

Stray cat playing in the parlor
Stray cat crying at my door
Is that you hiding in the garden
Cat, you don't come here anymore
You just ain't coming here any more

A SPELL FOR FELICIA,
THAT SHE COME AWAY

out of her
dusty windowless basement where her chick
sleeps in a coffin & babies
run bareassed thru the debris eating chocolate and kids
maybe 16 look tough tie up
in the gloom, and then rushing and in repose become
"hallucinated angels" of Vienna Boys Choir singing
Mozart Requiem to *my* youth, fifteen years
ago, requiem it is, she ties a
hawk's wing onto your shoulder, claps an
orange hat on her head, has
nine puppies somewhere, loses one, turns over
bloodstones in her hands, barefooted girls
walk in weeping and selling acid, a hot blue triumph sits
in front of the place, the altar is syringes
& black velvet & imitation leopard
watch straps: how pry her loose
from that, suck the essence from honeysuckle, or more like
the kernel out of a peach pit, bitter and tasting
of strychnine. . .

DEE'S SONG

Velvet lady, lay on velvet pillows
    in a house where the rain came in
Eucalyptus trees outside the velvet windows
    long silver fingers talking in the wind
Her eyes on the TV, her hair on a pillow
    horse in her arm, making gold
The lady was smiling, her thoughts ebbed and billowed
    her smokedreams were tapestry old

            The wooden house stood in a madrone grove
            Inside it were mirrors of glass
            And candlestick niches, and storybook dishes
            And vases of pewter and brass

California lady, slim and stylish as a leopard
    her tie-dye velvets lying on a shelf
Walking to her mailbox, airy-hearted as a shepherd-
    ess to find the smack she shoots into herself
Old man's gone south again in search of bread and glory powder
    eating percodan in all that canyon sun
The lady wears blue rhinestones and her magic doesn't flounder:
    target practice with a tin can and a gun

            The wooden house stood in a madrone grove
            Inside it were mirrors of glass
            And candlestick niches, and storybook dishes
            And vases of pewter and brass

Iridescent lady talking horoscopes and witches
　　cooking oatmeal porridge in the morning cold
Reading dirty tarot cards and washing painted dishes
　　while the ferns at your door fall to mold
And mushrooms are growing as big as your fist
　　and the skyscrapers teeter and sway
And the wraiths in your woodswamp all tell you to cool it
　　but then, that was never your way

　　　　　O lady I hope you have ice in your heart
　　　　　And the steel in your eyes is at rest
　　　　　They've locked you away for ten years and a day
　　　　　For the judge and the jury know best

There's dust on your candles, and wind in your bedroom
　　eats perfume you used in your hair
Your filched Goodwill wardrobe is scattered thru crash pads
　　where younger girls look for their share
You longed for a baby, a green-eyed madonna
　　whose swaddling clothes bundle the night
The stars drew your circle, like marshlights they mock you
　　my sister in a cage, sleep tight

MAGICK IN THEORY & PRACTICE

for Mike Goldberg

to all you with gaunt cheeks who sit
glamourized by the sounds of art in the
last remaining lofts, shining like gold in ore in the
sleek grime of NYC under the shadow
of MOMA, breathing no air, finding lustre in the
huge speaking canvases that whisper
like Miles Davis in your dusty ears, to all
you climbing laboriously on scaffolding shaping
these same canvases, bending light, or drinking hot plate
coffee on "studio couches" flanked by skinny girls
oh how my love reaches for you, gross & holy men
fancy women   pretty boys   expensive flowers   oh home
I may never see again   oh glamour
like Baudelaire fading in a long hall of mirrors
called past as I move backwards over
its black velvet floor

CANTICLE OF ST. JOAN

for Robert Duncan

1

It is in God's hands. How can I *decide*
France shall be free? And yet, with the clear song
of thrush, of starling, comes the word, decide
For human agency is freely chosen. I embrace
the iron crown, the nettle shirt, as I
embraced our lord god in the darkling wood
He of the silver hooves and flashing mane
Who shall be nameless.
Nameless as spruce and holly, which endure.
Holy St. Michael, but the ace of swords
is bitter! And the grail
not to be drunk, but carried into shelter.
The dragon, my naga, purrs, it lays its claws
about the bars which will soon close around me.
I stand in its breath, that fire, and read love
in its eyes like crystal balls which mirror gore
of the burning, pillaged cities I set free.
O brew me mistletoe, unveil the well
I shall lie down again with him who must be nameless
and sink my strong teeth into unhuman flesh.

2

Blessed be the holy saints, now and forever.
Blessed be Margaret & Brigit
Blessed be spruce & fir.
The sacred waterfall, Diana's bath, the wind
which brings iron clouds.
They fly out of the sea to the north, they recommend
that I wear woman's dress, they do not see
that I am Luci-fer, light bearer, lead & I follow
Mother, Sara-la-Kali, sacred Diana, I could have borne
a babe to our sovereign god, but would not
in this captivity, this blood
on my hands and no other
BUT SAINT GEORGE I WILL CONQUER
dragonslayer
who seeks to destroy the light in this holy forest
the yellow men call Europe

3

Where is my helmet? Battle
is what I crave, shock of lance, death cry, the air
filled with the jostling spirits of the dead,
meat & drink, the earth enriched with brain & entrail
horses' hooves sliding, the newly fallen
finding soft soggy bed on the fallen leaves, tears are too light
for this, GRAIL IS BLOOD IS HOLLY
red with our sorrow as we reclaim the ground
free to lie again with the horned man, the overlords
must build their edifices elsewhere, here we stomp
in our wooden shoes on the bare earth, take in our arms
boughs of the great trees, the misty fabrics of wee folk
flesh of our brethren, soon to grow cold, the children
half imp who live on earth as it were hell, I hear
the Voice, it bids me seek no forgiveness for none
is my share, my blessing is leaden sky, the sacred blood
of the children of forest shines like jewels
upon it.

4

O am I salamander, do I dance or leap
with pain, can I indeed fall & falling
fall out of this fire?   half charred to smoulder
black under blackening sky, the god is good
who made the stake strong, made the chains strong, I laugh
I think I laugh I hear peals of unholy laughter
like bells. The cross was ours before you holy men, its secret
there, where the two sticks meet, you cannot fathom.
I hear the cart creak home that brought me, the driver
won't even stay for this end—leap, pirouette.
Inside the grail is fire, the deep draught
melted rubies, blood of the most high god
whose name is Satan, and whose planet earth
I reclaim for the Bundschuh, sons of men.
My hair is burning and the mist is blue
which cracks my brain, I am not in the flame, I am the flame
the sun pours down, the Voice is a mighty roar
O little children's bones! the sword & cup
are shivered into stars.

REVOLUTIONARY LETTERS

(dedicated to Bob Dylan)

1

I have just realized that the stakes are myself
I have no other
ransom money, nothing to break or barter but my life
my spirit measured out, in bits, spread over
the roulette table, I recoup what I can
nothing else to shove under the nose of the *maitre de jeu*
nothing to thrust out the window, no white flag
this flesh all I have to offer, to make the play with
this immediate head, what it comes up with, my move
as we slither over this Go board, stepping always
(we hope) between the lines

4

Left to themselves people
grow their hair.
Left to themselves they
take off their shoes.
Left to themselves they make love
sleep easily
share blankets, dope & children
they are not lazy or afraid
they plant seeds, they smile, they
speak to one another. The word
coming into its own: touch of love
on the brain, the ear.

We return with the sea, the tides
we return as often as leaves, as numerous
as grass, gentle, insistent, we remember
the way
our babes toddle barefoot thru the cities of the universe.

12

the vortex of creation is the vortex of destruction
the vortex of artistic creation is the vortex of self destruction
the vortex of political creation is the vortex of flesh destruction
    flesh is in the fire, it curls and terribly warps
    fat is in the fire, it drips and sizzling sings
    bones are in the fire
        they crack tellingly in
        subtle hierglyphs of oracle
    charcoal singed
    the smell of your burning hair
for every revolutionary must at last will his own destruction
rooted as he is in the past he sets out to destroy

29

beware of those
who say we are the beautiful losers
who stand in their long hair and wait to be punished
who weep on beaches for our isolation

we are not alone: we have brothers in all the hills
we have sisters in the jungles and in the ozarks
we even have brothers on the frozen tundra
they sit by their fires, they sing, they gather arms
they multiply: they will reclaim the earth

nowhere we can go but they are waiting for us
no exile where we will not hear welcome home
'goodmorning brother, let me work with you
goodmorning sister, let me
fight by your side'

36

who is the we, who is
the they in this thing, did
we or they kill the indians, not me
my people brought here, cheap labor to exploit
a continent for them, did we
or they exploit it? do you
admit complicity, say '*we*
have to get out of Vietnam, *we* really should
stop poisoning the water, etc.' look closer, look again,
secede, declare your independence, don't accept
a share of the guilt *they* want to lay on *us*
MAN IS INNOCENT & BEAUTIFUL & born
to perfect bliss they envy, heavy deeds
make heavy hearts and to *them*
life is suffering. stand clear.

54

HOW TO BECOME A WALKING ALCHEMICAL EXPERIMENT

eat *mercury* (in wheat & fish)
breathe *sulphur* fumes (everywhere)
take plenty of (macrobiotic) *salt*
& cook the mixture in the heat
of an atomic explosion

68
LIFE CHANT

may it come that all the radiances
will be known as our own radiance
—Tibetan Book of the Dead

cacophony of small birds at dawn
        may it continue
sticky monkey flowers on bare brown hills
        may it continue
bitter taste of early miner's lettuce
        may it continue
music on city streets in the summer nights
        may it continue
kids laughing on roofs on stoops on the beach in the snow
        may it continue
triumphal shout of the newborn
        may it continue
deep silence of great rainforests
        may it continue
fine austerity of jungle peoples
        may it continue
rolling fuck of great whales in turquoise ocean
        may it continue
clumsy splash of pelican in smooth bays
        may it continue
astonished human eyeball squinting thru aeons at astonished
                          nebulae who squint back
        may it continue
clean snow on the mountain
        may it continue
fierce eyes, clear light of the aged
        may it continue
rite of birth & of naming
        may it continue

rite of instruction
        may it continue
rite of passage
        may it continue
love in the morning, love in the noon sun
love in the evening among crickets
        may it continue
long tales by fire, by window, in fog, in dusk on the mesa
        may it continue
love in thick midnight, fierce joy of old ones loving
        may it continue
the night music
        may it continue
grunt of mating hippo, giraffe, foreplay of snow leopard
                screeching of cats on the backyard fence
        may it continue
without police
        may it continue
without prisons
        may it continue
without hospitals, death medicine: flu & flu vaccine
        may it continue
without madhouses, marriage, highschools that are prisons
        may it continue
without empire
        may it continue
in sisterhood
        may it continue
thru the wars to come
        may it continue
in brotherhood
        may it continue
tho the earth seem lost
        may it continue

thru exile & silence
> may it continue

with cunning & love
> may it continue

as woman continues
> may it continue

as breath continues
> may it continue

as stars continue
> may it continue

> *may the wind deal kindly w/us*
> *may the fire remember our names*
> *may springs flow, rain fall again*
> *may the land grow green, may it swallow our mistakes*

we begin the work
> may it continue

the great transmutation
> may it continue

a new heaven & a new earth
> may it continue
> may it continue

TASSAJARA, 1969

Even Buddha is lost in this land
the immensity
takes us all with it, pulverizes, & takes us in

Bodhidharma came from the west.
Coyote met him

INFLUENCE (WOOING)

I am no
good at pleading, too proud and
awkward, my hands
know better how to ask, but how
w/you so distant, look the leaves
are gold, remember August they were
green and we lay under them on earth

now we dwell
under roofs, we lie
side by side w/out touching
when I am
alone, my tears drop
thinking of winter

BEFORE COMPLETION

like wind, dispersing, like some huge
blood offering to the North American landscape
we are being eaten, our puny
European arts ground to powder as the Rockies
erode, the desert
spreads to the sea

FOR BLAKE

by now it is too late to wonder
why we are wherever we are
(tho some peace is possible): singing on the breath
& we have had bodies of Fire and lived on the Sun
& we have had bodies of Water and lived on Venus
and bodies of Air that screeched as they tore around Jupiter
all our eyes remembering Love

TO THE SPECTRE OF THE LECTURER,
LONG DEAD

Why it shd all
come clear to me now: betrayal
I sit here, elbows
      leaning on thighs
legs spread, stomach hangs thru them
full, slightly painful
     I look at
the flesh my hands are: thinking
you probably havent aged/
       at all,
   I wd be ashamed
to face you: lines
      around my eyes
low breasts &, just now
bigbelly for the fifth time, I go
over it, in this S. F. room,
       big fog
coming in, grey sky, grey street, shouts
of black kids, playing late, now
8 yrs after & for the first time it comes as pain
comes clear
    what I walked out on
To turn one's back on love
       & walk away
like Casablanca,
     I hear the roar
of yr pain/ my pain that I never
touched, or acknowledged,
       my hands
pressed over eyelids, hair short too
not at all
    what you remember

PRAYER TO THE MOTHERS

they say you lurk here still, perhaps
in the depths of the earth or on
some sacred mountain, they say
you walk (still) among men, writing signs
in the air, in the sand, warning warning weaving
the crooked shape of our deliverance, anxious
not hasty. Careful. You step among cups, step out of
crystal, heal with the holy glow of your
dark eyes, they say you unveil
a green face in the jungle, wear blue
in the snows, attend on
births, dance on our dead, croon, fuck, embrace
our weariness, you lurk here still, mutter
in caves, warn, warn & weave
warp of our hope, link hands against
the evil in the stars, O rain
poison upon us, acid which eats clean
wake us like children from a nightmare, give the slip
to the devourers whom I cannot name
the metal men who walk
on all our substance, crushing flesh
to swamp

*

friend

tonight in the rain

I am afraid to hear

your songs

TO MY FATHER

In my dreams you stand among roses.
You are still the fine gardener you were.
You worry about mother.
You are still the fierce wind, the intolerable force
that almost broke me.
Who forced my young body into awkward and proper clothes
Who spoke of his standing in the community.
And men's touch is still a little absurd to me
because you trembled when you touched me.
What external law were you expounding?
How can I take your name like prayer?
My youngest son has your eyes.
Why are you knocking at the doors of my brain?
You kept all their rules and more.
What were you promised that you cannot rest?
What fierce, angry honesty in the darkness?
What can you hope who had preferred my death
to the birth of my oldest daughter?
O fierce hummer of tunes
Forget, eat the black seedcake.
In my dreams you stand at the door of your house
and weep for your wife, my mother.

TO TARA

Rosebud, or fat baby cougar bending
Over the page, rising like breath, a
smile, a grace, in passage, like the swans
waking at midnight in a watery garden

She raises slow plump arms, she spins
Solemn as conch, the ritual
Winks, among cypresses

AND VERCHIEL

His name is almost on my lips.
He stands before me glowing, a young
man with a sword. I can glimpse
gardens over his shoulder where stars
bloom. He is
someone I almost know:

adepts
who also sing
are found rarely in the
Western tradition

PRAYER TO THE ANCESTORS

O you who burn forever wheeling
like stars across our night, thin hands
like flame held in the winds & the winds too
burning oh you gauntlegged travellers of roads
too rough for us who saw
the stars on fire blooming & going out, who hear
& heard the angels of apocalypse before
we even charred the earth, who tremble (forever)
on the brink of some
unthinkable liberation, who almost
stepped out of time & took us too, you bend
thin holy faces earthward, lean
gaunt shapely bellies, follow on bony feet
the ends of your hair all burning, can you
break time like a shell, break sentience, lead us
to Glory now (the depths
of space a single sheet of flame. . .

TWO FROM GALLUP

1
SAD IN GALLUP

Motel row: sidewalk along
66; new sandals hurting
big wind coming up. Hungry
for grain, for touch of my
children, I chant
sandy Heart Sutra to
Indian graveyard behind
pastel trailer camp: the Santa Fe
Railroad joins in.

2
HORNY IN GALLUP I think
of going to bed w/an Indian,
any Indian, but I have no car, I'm
tired, don't know
any Indians, afraid I'll get
rolled, so I think
of you. On the phone you say
you are typing a catalogue, you say
the food stamps havent come, you dont say
you miss me, you sound
the full thousand & more miles
away

FRAGMENTED ADDRESS TO THE FBI

O do you in fedora or trenchcoat bear record
Of the elusive days, date & hour
The subway journeys to forgotten loves
(Do you indeed have them forever, name & picture)
The old phone numbers, whose rhythm no longer
Sings for us, descriptions of long dead cars?
O gentle chroniclers of our rainbow lives
Blessed laborers in the labyrinthine archive
Recording angels who will consign to fire
Name & form, body & papers while we
Rise singing above the trees

LETTER TO JEANNE (at Tassajara)

dry heat of the Tassajara canyon
moist warmth of San Francisco summer
bright fog reflecting sunrise as you
step out of September zendo
heart of your warmth, my girl, as you step out
into your vajra pathway, glinting
like your eyes turned sideways at us
your high knowing 13-year-old
wench-smile, flicking your thin
ankles you trot toward Adventure
all sizes & shapes, O may it be various
for you as for me it was, sparkle
like dustmotes at dawn in the back
of grey stores, like the shooting stars
over the Hudson, wind in the Berkshire pines

O you have landscapes dramatic like mine
never was, uncounted caves
to mate in, my scorpio, bright love
like fire light up your beauty years
on these new, jagged hills

*
I say my new name
over and over
coming home from the temple

AMERICAN INDIAN ART:
FORM AND TRADITION

Were we not fine
were we not all fine
in our buckskin coats, the quillwork, the
buttons & beads?
Were we not fine
were we not all fine

O they have hung our
empty shirts in their cold
marble halls. They have
labeled our baskets, lighted
our masks, disassembled our pipes
in glass cases.

       (We flashed in those colors
thru the dark woods over the dun plains
in the harsh desert)
       Where
do they hang our breath? our
bright glance, where is our song now
our sorrow?

Walker Art Center, Minneapolis

TAKEOFF, FLIGHT 347

goodbye to
mountains of agate, amber, magic
bauxite, brittle secret
alchemy texts. Goodbye angels
on Johnny Dodd's ceiling, indians
staring out from his walls, red plastic
devil on red brick wall. Mysterious
wet streets, cobblestones, platforms, broken trucks
lost theatres, 3 a.m. cocaine, burning
purity of line, young men
naked in raggy blankets on scraps
of foam rubber, intellectual roaches, slobs, ballet boys, despairing
kids in strollers. Dirty windows, stairs, halls, grimy sheets
pure filth in nostrils, endline song
of jazz & dervish & Callas on stereo. Wind
full of dust, goodbye!   bright
gilded skyline, gilded dust, brown
burning smog like atomized shit, dead river
I love & will, forever, A.I.R.
on all those broken doors, eyeholes, police locks, bells
that never work.
Mysterious fashions fading into rags.
Diamonds that transmute themselves to rhinestones.
sun city w/no sun, big apple wormy now
& covered w/soft brown spots. The lingering hope
looks out of boyish eyes of balding faggots, hums
thru the accents of the garment district, turns
in the sooty ghetto. For a while
you are/ or were, hub
o' the universe, dreams
fell on you from distant constellations, songs
finished now, still stir your air, goodbye
ghost hometown fatherland *der heimat,* bright stars
of windows lighting nothing, looking out
on strikers in the rain.

SIXTH NOTEBOOK INCANTATION

Ping-ponging back & forth across America
starting small grass fires where I land
in Minnesota jail, Wyoming
community college, high schools of South Tucson
may I always remember the Bodhisattvas
sitting down in BIA cafeteria, may I
cut hamburger with the sword of Manjusri
pluck lotuses on windy Nebraska hills
set jewels of Lokeshvara round my neck
after I brush my teeth in steam-heated
dormitory bathroom.
Pure light of ancient wisdom, stay w/me
like a follow spot, pierce my
                    armored heart, clean
cobwebs of plastic food & deadened
                    eternal sorrow.
"How do you like it here?" "I like it
very much."

MINNESOTA MORNING ODE

for Giordano Bruno

The City of the Sun is coming! I hear it! I smell it!
here, where they have made even the earth a jailer
where not even the shadows of animals sneak over the land
where children are injured & taught to apologize for their scars
the City of the Sun cannot be far now—

(that's what you said then, brother, waiting in prison
eight years to be burned, to find the sun at last
on the Campo de Fiori—FIELD OF FLOWERS— yes)
how could it be far?
isn't evil at its peak?
(you asked 300 years ago) has not
the descent into matter reached a nadir? & here
5000 miles later, Northern Minnesota
a forest once, now wasteland
where they mow grass, rake leaves:

I vomit lies like the rest, not knowing
whom to trust, here where betrayal is taught as virtue
I weep alone for the words I would like to say
& silently put the faces of the old gods
into the hands of the children; hope they recognize them
here in this Christian place, where Christ the Magus
& Christ the Healer are both forgotten, where the veil
of the temple is rent, but no resurrection follows. . .

THE CITY OF THE SUN comes soon, cannot be far
yes, you are right—what's a millennium
or two to us, brother? The gods can wait
they are strong, they rise—the golden tower
flashing the light of planets, the speaking statues
that guard its four gates, the holy wind
that carries the spirit of heaven down thru the stars

104

it is here! it is here!
I will build it
on this spot. I will build it at Attica
& Wounded Knee
on the Campo de Fiori, at the Vatican:
the strong, bright light of flesh which is the link
the laughter, which transmutes

Minnesota Home School
Sauk Centre

BRIEF WYOMING MEDITATION

I read
Sand Creek massacre: White Antelope's scrotum
                              became tobacco pouch
for Colorado Volunteer;
I see
destitute prairie: short spiny grass & dusty wind
& all for beef too expensive to eat;
I remember
at least two thirds of you voted for madman Nixon
were glad to bomb the "gooks" in their steamy jungle
& I seek
    I seek
    I seek
the place where your nature meets mine,
          the place where we touch

        nothing lasts long
        nothing
                but earth
        & the mountains

TARA

1
on the airplane she said
"I feel stretched"
where? I asked & she laid her hand
on her crown cakra

2
this morning we walked to breakfast
birds were singing
"HOLY HOLY HOLY HOLY" she whispered
"that's what they're saying
HO-WHEE   HO-WHEE
WHOLE WHEAT
well, anyway whole wheat
is holy too"

TRAVELING, AGAIN

Tacoma Airport. I am met by poet-in-residence. Tall as in
            art council description, but where is the long blonde hair?
It is mousy brown & cut just below the ears.
If that is long hair in Tacoma, I've got something to worry about.
All the way into town I am watching the sky: it is lurid orange; result
of clouds & smog.

I am installed in five-story Motor Hotel
with a fine view of smokestacks polluting sky & bay. This is
            downtown Tacoma! We go for coffee
at a miserable greasy-spoon called Vern's.
One derelict at the counter, talking to himself. Waitress sweeping,
            getting ready to close.
The quaintness of grim America is lost on me.— I've seen it
            too many times? It's grimmer than quaint;

The young poet w/me proceeds to describe w/relish
how he was almost mugged in Kansas City. I want to shout
PAUL, THE QUAINTNESS OF GRIM AMERICA IS LOST—
but I listen & nod. He is from Denver. He tells me why all
            my poet friends in Denver
will never make it. He avoids mentioning
that they are all junkies, that's why they'll never make it.
He speaks w/disdain of the beat jargon they write in
& I mentally check out my poems: wd he like them? He wdnt.

But *they*—they are noisy & junkies, they have guns
slung over their armchairs; they listen to King Pleasure records
while writing those out-of-date poems & I sit in Vern's
& long to be in their warm & chaotic houses, snorting coke
going out in the mountain dark to talk to sleepy horses
shoot all the Milky Way into my arm

But the grimness of this quaint America is too much
for my skinny new friend here & we discuss something safe
like the weather, or William Stafford, and walk on back.

RAMADA INN, DENVER

It's taken a whole day to get from Great Falls to Casper
& I ain't there yet!
White fog envelopes Great Falls, envelopes
"nearly everything up to Banff," one old Canadian
tells me as we bump along on a bus
to Helena, where we take a plane to Salt Lake, arrive late, get on
(late) plane to Denver, arrive late, discover plane
to Casper has left without us.

Western Airlines puts us up at Ramada Inn.
I am too crazed to sleep; take my last seven dollars
& make it to the bar.
The only remaining barstool is in between
a rancher from Montana & a blonde semi-longhair in a suit
probably just out of college. I order a margarita & listen.

Turns out the rancher is really a rancher, but the blonde
thinks he's James Bond or something. He's a narc
what works w/customs for the airforce in Thailand.
He is a great admirer of Thailand, tells me
that Bangkok is at least as modern as Rapid City.
He is a great admirer of Thailand women
who are content to fuck for peanuts & beer
or clean & cook for forty-five dollars a month.
He just left his wife in Great Falls cause she was pregnant
& that won't do in Thailand. He's on his way
to San Anton' to pick up two marijuana dogs
(in her stead?) I want to ask him but I don't.
I'm drinking my second margarita & scared to open my mouth
lest I shd drunkenly make the guy suspicious
& he shd bring his dogs to sniff the crack under my door.

He is coming on strong & liberal: tells me how stupid
he feels sitting all day at the airport w/a dog at the end of a leash
smelling suitcases. "When the dog gets something we tear the
                    luggage apart."
He's proud, in a liberal way, he wants me to know
he carries no gun, just handcuffs & mace, he denounces dope
while getting drunker & drunker.

My second margarita was on the rocks.
I crack the ice cubes nervously between my teeth.
The rancher's wife comes in, thank god, she has the art
of playing Silly Woman—she giggles & says
she'd *much* rather live in Glacier than Bangkok; the rancher
beams proudly at her. They both drink beer. I love them
madly & drunkenly. I cleverly maneuver off my barstool
bid everyone goodnight. Blondie seems disappointed—
I maybe forgot to tell him I don't like peanuts?
He offers another drink, but I grin wickedly at him
                    & tell him lewdly
"No thanks, I'm just drunk enough for a nice hot bath."
& walk what I hope is a straight line to the door.

NARROW PATH INTO THE BACK COUNTRY

for Audre Lorde

1

You are flying to Dahomey, going back
to some dream, or never-never land
more forbidding & perfect
than Oz. Will land in Western airport
noisy, small & tacky, will look around
for Oshun, as she stands
waiting for baggage. Well, we carry
pure-land paradise within, you carry
it to Dahomey, from Staten Island.

2

we endure. this we are certain of. no more.
we endure: famine, depression, earthquake,
     pestilence, war, flood, police state,
     inflation
ersatz food. burning cities. you endure,
     I endure. It is written
on the faces of our children. Pliant, persistent
     joy; Will like mountains, hope
that batters yr heart & mine. (Hear them shout)
And I will not bow out, cannot see
your war as different. Turf stolen from
     yours & mine; clandestine magics
we practice, all of us, for their protection.
That they have fruit to eat & rice & fish
till they grow strong.

(Remember the octopus we did not cook
Sicilian style/West African style—it fills
your daughter's dream)   I refuse
to leave you to yr battles, me to mine

my girl
chased white coyote, sister to my wolf
& not thru mesas.

3
how to get the food on the table
how to heal
what survives this whirlwind:
people and land. The sea
tosses feverish; screams in delirium.
To have the right herb drying in the kitchen:
your world & mine/ all others: not the Third
this is Fourth World going down, the Hopi say.
Yet we endure.

4
And more, we fly to light, fly into
pure-land paradise, New York
Dahomey, Mars, Djakarta, Wales
The willful, stubborn children carrying seed
all races; hurtling time & space & stars
to find container large & fine enough
fine-wrought enough for our joy.
For all our joy.

THE BANQUET

Your face is craggy as the Marin County hills
Ravaged yr eyes where meteorites
               fell thru yr face
And yr skin smooth as waves
Flutters against my palm
Moves small
           terror
              fills you
I suck
      yr terror into my gut
I suck
      yr passion
I drink yr tears

In the dry places I find yr anger
hard as stone.
It shines like steel
I cannot move against it.

I reach deep into you.
I pull it out. Your anger
      as large as your fist
We look at it together, lying there
      my thigh
Is against yr stomach. I want to sing
      "O woman shapely as a swan
         on yr account
         I shall not die"

And the smooth stone from yr gut
Gleams on the pillow between us.

BACKYARD

where angels turned into honeysuckle & poured nectar into my mouth
where I french-kissed the roses in the rain
where demons tossed me a knife to kill my father in the stark
       simplicity of the sky
where I never cried
where all the roofs were black
where no one opened the venetian blinds
O Brooklyn! Brooklyn!
where fences crumbled under the weight of rambling roses
and naked plaster women bent eternally white over birdbaths
the icicles on the chains of the swings tore my fingers
& the creaking tomato plants tore my heart as they wrapped their
       roots around fish heads rotting beneath them
& the phonograph too creaked Caruso come down from the skies;
       Tito Gobbi in gondola; Gigli ridiculous in soldier uniform;
       Lanza frenetic
& the needle tore at the records & my fingers
tore poems into little pieces & watched the sky
where clouds torn into pieces & livid w/neon or rain
scudded away from Red Hook, away from Gowanus Canal, away
from Brooklyn Navy Yard where everybody worked, to fall to pieces
       over Clinton Street
and the plaster saints in the yard never looked at the naked women
       in the birdbaths
and the folks coming home from work in pizza parlor or furniture
       store, slamming wrought iron gates to come
       upon brownstone houses,
never looked at either: they saw that the lawns were dry
were eternally parched beneath red gloomy sunsets we viewed from
       a thousand brownstone stoops
leaning together by thousands on the same
wrought-iron bannister, watching the sun impaled
on black St. Stephen's steeple

FOR PIGPEN

Velvet at the edge of the tongue,
at the edge of the brain, it was
velvet.   At the edge of history.

Sound was light. Like tracing
ancient letters w/yr toe on the
floor of the ballroom.
They came & went, hotel guests
like the Great Gatsby.
And wondered at the music.
                    Sound was light.

jagged sweeps of discordant
Light. Aurora borealis over
some cemetery. A bark. A howl.

At the edge of history & there was
                    no time

shouts.   trace circles
of breath. All futures. Time
was this light & sound
spilled out of it.

                    Flickered
& fell under blue windows. False dawn.
And too much wind.

                    We come round.
Make circles. Blank as a clock.
Spill velvet damage on the edge
of history.

AN EXERCISE IN LOVE

for Jackson Allen

My friend wears my scarf at his waist
I give him moonstones
He gives me shell & seaweeds
He comes from a distant city & I meet him
We will plant eggplants & celery together
He weaves me cloth

      Many have brought the gifts
      I use for his pleasure
      silk, & green hills
      & heron the color of dawn

My friend walks soft as a weaving on the wind
He backlights my dreams
He has built altars beside my bed
I awake in the smell of his hair & cannot remember
his name, or my own.

NO PROBLEM PARTY POEM

first glass broken on patio no problem
forgotten sour cream for vegetables no problem
Lewis MacAdam's tough lower jaw no problem
cops arriving to watch bellydancer no problem
plastic bags of melted ice no problem
wine on antique tablecloth no problem
scratchy stereo no problem
neighbor's dog no problem
interviewer from Berkeley Barb no problem
absence of more beer no problem
too little dope no problem
leering Naropans no problem
cigarette butts on the altars no problem
Marilyn vomiting in planter box no problem
Phoebe renouncing love no problem
Lewis renouncing Phoebe no problem
hungry ghosts no problem
absence of children no problem
heat no problem
dark no problem
arnica scattered in nylon rug no problem
ashes in bowl of bleached bones & juniper berries no problem
lost Satie tape no problem
loss of temper no problem
arrogance no problem
boxes of empty beer cans & wine bottles no problem
thousands of styrofoam cups no problem
Gregory Corso no problem
Allen Ginsberg no problem
Diane di Prima no problem
Anne Waldman's veins no problem
Dick Gallup's birthday no problem
Joanne Kyger's peyote & rum no problem

wine no problem
coca-cola no problem
getting it on in the wet grass no problem
running out of toilet paper no problem
decimation of pennyroyal no problem
destruction of hair clasp no problem
paranoia no problem
claustrophobia no problem
growing up on Brooklyn streets no problem
growing up in Tibet no problem
growing up in Chicano Texas no problem
bellydancing certainly no problem
figuring it all out no problem
giving it all up no problem
giving it all away no problem
devouring everything in sight no problem
                    what else in Allen's refrigerator?
                    what else in Anne's cupboard?
                    what do you know that you
                           haven't told me yet?
no problem.   no problem.   no problem.

staying another day no problem
getting out of town no problem
telling the truth, almost no problem
                  easy to stay awake
                  easy to go to sleep
                  easy to sing the blues
                  easy to chant sutras
what's all the fuss about?

it decomposes—no problem
we pack it in boxes—no problem
we swallow it with water, lock it in the trunk,
   make a quick getaway. NO PROBLEM.

THE FIRE GUARDIAN

Let yrself be seen as shadow
    in the light
or as a thin lens   color does not
pass thru
no yellow glow   no blue
    fierce purpose
this spilling liquid caught
    in vase of flesh

pours over as sight, as touch
    it is light
interlaced w/light makes these
    worlds bud
tensile web   eye to eye
    skin smooth
as spider's belly, tentative
    & ecstatic as lizards

on crumbling sandstone molecules
    which dance
in their sudden, expected brains
    like stars
thru ponderosa dance in ours
    when we fall to sleep
on bed of needles in the arms
    of our own black pain & wake
cresting again, riding invisible
    soul-stuff   (we call it
joy

FOR H.D.

1

trophies of pain I've gathered.   whose sorrow
do I shore up, in trifles?   the weavings,
paintings, jewels, plants, I bought

with my heart's hope.   rocks from the road
to Hell, broken pieces of statuary, ropes,
bricks, from the city of Dis.

encrusted.   they surround me: nest
the horror of each act from which I saved
a dried, dismembered hand.   poisoned

amulets, empty vials still fuming.   their tears
saved lovingly as my own.   to have
"lived passionately"   this secret

hoarding of passion.   Truth turned against itself.

2

Heart's truth, spat out of sleep, was only hate.
I caught it, on my pillows.   Tried
to turn it to diamonds.   Sometimes succeeded

so far as quartz in the hand.   Like ice it melted.
Heat of my will   burns down the walls around me
time after time.   Yet there remain

encrustations of old loves.   Filthy barnacles
sucking my marrow.   My illness:
that I am not blind,   yet cannot transmute

In body cauldron I carried
hate or indifference, anger,   clothed it
in child flesh,   & in the light

it seemed I had worked magic. But the stone
sticks in their throats. Night screams & morning tears
phantoms of fathers,   dead skin hung on

old bones.   Like jewels in the hair.

3
"I am a woman of pleasure"   & give back
salt for salt. Untrammeled by hope or knowledge
I have left these

in the grindstones of other thresholds.   Now only bedrock
basalt to crack your breath. Beloved.   To suck for drink.
I am not fair. But you are more than fair.

You are too kind. Still water   in which,
like a crystal, the phantoms dance.
Each carrying death like a spear,   for we die

of each other's hate, or indifference.   Draw blood
to draw out poison.   But it has seat
in heart of our heart, the hollow of the marrow

of our bones.   Salt for salt   & the desert
is infinite   it drinks
more juice than we carry.

4

O, I'd yet beg bread, or water,   wd lie
in the dry wash & pray the flood wd come
That my eyes unstick,   that I see stars

as I drown.   For 25 years, bruised, wounded,
I've hid in rocks.   Fed by hyenas, vultures, the despised
that chew carrion   & share the meal

which, sharing,   you lose caste;   forget
human laws.   My blood
tastes in my mouth like sand.

5

humiliated   time & again   by song
laughter from cracked lips.
power of incantation stirring to life

what shd sleep, like stone.   yet the turquoise
sparkles.   "happy to see you"   stars
beat against my skin.   what is mine:

cold prickles,   moving out
from spine.   pulsing skull
pushing to light.   burning bushes

that lie.   snow mountains where gods
leave laws, like stones.   Anubis in Utah.
and tears.   and tears.   and tears.

to bless my desert   and give back
song for salt.

THE CLEARING IN AUTUMN

1
Hot sun & cold wind. Bank of fog sits
on Inverness hills. Looming. Hasnt moved for hours.
Desultory birds with unmusical chirps. Excitement in the sounds
        of water:
crisp separateness of each wave you never hear
in summer.   I love you & it is OK
that this leads me on strange paths. (Crispness of each wave)
        It has also given me
larger notebook, two pens, sun in the clearing.
(Those three lines for Jackson.) Crow, trilling, flies into
the sun. Tart sweetness of time
white butterfly. Wild roses that smell like cherries
Scrawny black flowers of hemlock like fallen stars.
Final blackberries, thistles, bundles of dry reeds.
"Without any irritable reaching after fact
and reason."

2
I seek to share, as otherwhere
changes of mood. To hear & see
buzz of autumn flies, drip of water
into the old tank, trembling
of seedpod on dry grass
with yr ears, yr eyes. Touch is superfluous
to this: shared acknowledgement
of the moment.
I spin it like a web of jewels between us. It is the substance
of Tomales Bay.

3

Those words for Jackson, though I know the form
another's. He is shadow cast
in flattened grass by One who himself
comes between me & the light. Defines light.
Colors it. Comrade Prism, angel form whose shadows
I love again & again. And do not grasp. Shining translator
of sunlight, lie here. Let me drink you.

4

That tree my angel. Wisps of cloud
his dance. Fogbank explosion of light in which
white egrets lift & fall, pelicans tumble.
Infinity of fog-mirrors in moonlight, mirrored back
by the Bay. Splintering universes. O
you are blue, you are golden, you fall on me
as cloud, you are starbody pressing
on stone circle, while Mother Astarte
peeks over hills & whistles. I want to say
Never leave me; want to say
Tell me your Name.

5

Is it for this I am salvaged, thus
thrown away. While taste of
kitchen garden, human sinew, hearth
slips past & I am solitary
in autumn hills, waiting angels

intangible Lovers I open my body to
inaudible cries as I spin toward
the sun

LIMANTOUR BEACH—I

Dark o' the moon, but
Just before dusk, the sun's out
Look, we have shadows

Dark o' the moon &
just before dusk, the sun's out
The waves change color

>   sun's out
>   almost down
>   waves go from grey
>   to blue/ & tonight
>   black:
>   dark o' the moon

sky foam: what wind?
what pulls
milky way's tides

gulls too fat to walk
us w/sand on our toes
& the sea's
pouring gold on the land

LIMANTOUR BEACH—II

surf riding in / spray torn off
the top. fierce manes of Poseidon's horses
outlined white against black; flying fog bank
sun sits poised above

& line of water cuts angles to the shore
where gulls line up, solemn
slumps of black / sunning
their backs.   3 pelicans fly low, clumsy

no longer in love, no longer
regretting love. pleased to have traded
particularity of pleasure (cloisonné of yr face
turned to mine)
                    for openness of space
play of light & shade on these hills.

kids building towers in the rising tide.

4 TAKES, SAME HAIKU

for Tigger Beauparlant

First storm of autumn
and the path is strewn
with fallen fuschia blossoms

Hummingbird seeking
the fallen fuschia blossoms:
first autumn storm

After this first storm
the hummingbirds mourn
fallen fuschias on wet ground

Fuschias broken on
wet ground; hummingbirds hungry
Autumn storms begin

1 MRN 38.30

1

some nights
I hear without straining
surf breaking at the Point
& I wear illusion lightly
striding toward a house that never was
from a studio whose outline
existed in eternity

2

moon rising late
smell of woodsmoke in my hair
my hands full of wistful paper portraits
                                of friends
whose shapes have dissolved

3

cold. orion rising
over black hills. surf pounding
inside my head, or out there?

TWO DREAM SONGS

1. Song of the Crab Spirit

The blue turns to gold
The gold does not fade
The gold becomes blue
The blue does not change

    Flecks of white
    In the dark:
    Pebbles in the sea
    Stars in the sky

2. Dream Love Song

Cotton-cloud woman
Flintstone woman
The wetness in your hair
Like dew in the grass

ANY DAY NOW

for Andrei Voznesensky

how do you love is the question, and who
and when it comes down from the sky, does it matter
father, friend, daughter; who/ do you love
is the question and where
is the time for this passion, will not emerge
from garden parties, when then
you do love, is it sudden and tough
do you love to love, is it
music, who
and how do you love, did you
love or not love & do you

THESE DAYS

for Bill Vitt

undisguisedly mirthful & given
to lavish dancing. Permanently
removed from concern abt my
kitchen. Love is a liquor that
warms the blood. It is useful
in that it stirs in me at dawn
& I see the mist burn off & the
waters still. Then the wind
rises. I don't call anyone, but
walk to the meadow w/Rudi.
We float narcissus & stare
at whitened wood. When
we return, love is rousing as the
good Celebes coffee I brew
the stoneware cup tingles rough
under my fingers. Elton John
gives way to Monk when Alex
gets up. There are white caps
on the Bay & love is a taste
in my mouth, a fur
of light on my eyes.
Perhaps I'll call you later.
Perhaps I'll bump
over yr dirt road & visit
with the children.

POEM OF REFUSALS

No strong men in shirtsleeves
striding thru
my kitchen: warm & obtuse.
No me curled-like-kitten around
a sleeping child & smiling
seductively.
No short skirts, no long
breaths; I will not
glance sidelong after reading a poem
to see
if you understood it.
No cozy patios, front yards
my cats
will never be fat. No one
will put me on a T-shirt;
I may never
learn to put on my own make-up.
Don' wanna sit
quiescent in the car while someone else
drives. No circles to go
around in. No checkerboard
linoleum. No.
No dishwasher; washing machine
unlikely. No flowers,
good legs, plaintive
poems about marriage. Wind
is what men are, & my poems
the sea. Children like grass
on the hills—they hang
in there. Or like a forest.
They don't come & go.
No rainbows. Only pelicans
flopping clumsy, hoping
for that one

Big Fish. You can bet
I wont be wistful, let it go by
wondering later what it *could* have been like.
My memories run together.
And I'm none too sure now
who did what to whom.
What we did wrong.
But I burned the script
where I meet your eyes & smile.

WYOMING SERIES

In October all the bodhisattvas come to Wyoming
they sleep beside the hunters in motels
they hover at daybreak by springs & waterholes
whispering warning to the antelope.

In October the hunters feel fine, they are warm w/blood
they are warm w/whiskey
                      & able to make love
once more to their women, who stroke them w/antlers
still red at the stump.
A wild excitement fills the men as they enter
They growl like mountain lion.
                          The women taste of blood
inside & out.

At dawn the bodhisattvas come to Wyoming
they stand beside motel beds, they gather fumes
of this angry loving
                    to turn to pure sorrow
silver elixir they catch in
                      crystal vials
to pour on the headless corpses of antelope
            in the folds of raw, harmonious hills.

       *   *   *

He said "never shoot a running antelope
even that much adrenalin
            poisons the delicate meat."

       *   *   *

Here lizard-woman works her tensile claws
into sands newly thrust
                    from sea-floor.

And time is a song the land sings.

*   *   *

He said   I have midwifed many deaths
she said   and I births.   She said
that is why in the old time   the female
was named Severity & the male
                              Mercy.
Midwife of death, you open the door of escape.

He said   it doesn't pay to eat antelope
unless you know to eat prana
                        instead of flesh.

*   *   *

This is a love poem to a harsh land.
In fall the air of Wyoming is full of angels
they are singing requiem to hunters' children
they are resurrecting paths
                        which cross the land
like shimmering lines.
The angels clean rifles, they wipe stains
from the floors of new Dodge campers; they mend baffles
in down bags; they brighten orange jackets & vests & caps
they lie in cold rivers
                        their wings crossed over their eyes.
They are singing requiem to hunters' children.

*   *   *

Lizard-woman knows what she's doing
                              she out in the night
bringing a message here, a warning here.
When the prairie is restless she does it by jumping
Star-to-star she jumps, tho she knows in the cold
her blood is supposed to be sluggish & she shd sleep.
The hieroglyphs need to be traced
                              on the stone walls.

           *   *   *

In Wyoming the lovers shelter out of the wind.
They huddle in doorways of broken motels.
They huddle in reservation shacks.
They weave them nests of promise:
                              spun glass & tankas.
They weave green plants & look at light thru the chinks.
They huddle in mining tents
                              & company towns
They weave into each other & make the dawn.

She said   "first birds
                        then trucks."
The light poured in.

           *   *   *

The buck stood in the stream & watched them break the lock. It
understood they were not hunters, so it stayed & watched while they
drilled out the lock from the trunk of the car. The deer knew about cars:
they hunted, but this one was still. The buck's eyes met the woman's
across the water.

           *   *   *

This is a love poem for women I never touched.
In Wyoming the bodhisattvas have turned to stone
We chip at them in canyons
                    by small streams.

        *   *   *

The woman was hunting / she thought she was hunting rocks.
She searched out crevices in the butte for lizards
Snow
        lay on the edges of things
Outlined the mountain.

The woman was harvesting rocks.
In the air above the water
The deer & the woman drank news
                        from each other's eyes.

        *   *   *

This is a love poem. For men who fell w/me
from sheer rock ledges, into tornadoes of breath.
The men in whose loneliness I encircle myself
In whose eye
        I explode.

        *   *   *

In Wyoming the Bodhisattvas have turned to stone
They stand like rock walls, they heave themselves from the earth
They tangle the roots of aspen in river canyons.
They are the megaliths set by hands so ancient
you could not say if they were flesh or spirit
God-power, or the giants walking soft.

In Wyoming the giants still sing in windy canyons.
The lovers hear them, it gives an edge to their dreams.

THE SPIRIT OF ROMANCE

> ... *in Gaelic* rūn *means both*
> *"mystery" & "the beloved"*
> —*Ezra Pound*

& we say "casting the Runes"
as if we cd talk
              to the Mystery
as if the Word
              were mystery
& the cast /
              of Divination
archaic & direct as
Love

    Oracle where we
are present to the Word
& cast of Light.
              Beloved.   Mystery.

LIGHT POEM

for Sheppard

Light on dry hayfields, the cedar
stark, nested in gullies, light
blank on smog wall, thrown, glaring, light
riding the mist as spray, at the end
of this city: ocean.
                  Light on
waves, on cement wall, light
like a passion at the back of the eyes.

Red and white lights of radio tower w/the moon
full, between, this light
on ten thousand faces in the sun.
The way light glints off sweat.
Blue light in a plastic pool.
Inner lit spaces, dusty colors transparent
    this pink, these greens
the golden backs of bees in the purple grapes.

Neon on wet streets. Flash of fish
in the waters. The Green Flash
split second of emerald sky. Aurora borealis
like a veil. Like a city of lights.

                          Amber gels flash
on saxophone; mikes red and yellow; green drums.
The Web of Light in the sky like a net of wrinkles
falling across the faces of loved poets.
Jellyfish light. Nitroglycerin brightness.
Lavender/pink sunset extending
clear to the east. Filling the sky out of which
an eternal moon. Is that citron?
How did you get
                those colors?

Light of the hand in action.
Light of the hair.
Gleam on the point of this pen as I write.
Diffused spaces of light in darkened rooms.
Sodium arc. Carbon
Magnesium / phosphorus.
Light in blue topaz distinct
        from lights of beryl.
Bubbles of light in the glass.

Light cased in sand grains, silica
light, copper light, iron light
brass polished / eärendil / light
of sirius, cygnus, flames
of driftwood blue w/sea salt.

The light of African masks, the
light of tundras;   dustmotes dancing
on gull's wing catching rose
light as the sun rises.

The light in the faces of bears, in the eyes
of spiders. Swamplight. Light out of Flanders.
Cigarettes in the dark. The light that pours
out of canvas and into the eye.

Sending the light of the eye out, into the world.
Touch of the gaze. Poured essence
                                thru the eye
you catch in an upturned cup:
yr eyes on mine.
                Light crackling around
the body.
        Field.

PROPHETISSA

Two from One
Three from Two
and out of the Three
the Four, as the first
                    —Maria the Prophet
                    (second-century alchemist)

Two from One:

know this wind as
                    fire.   Flame
at the heart of stone.
                    Leaping arc
from black dwarf star that spins
the double helix.   And know

this fire as talk.   The word.
Bursting in cunt or asshole
                            bursting
in cupped & tensing mouth
                            The
fucking word.   Heartfire of stars as they
circle & lean toward touch
                            hold orbit
spiraling
            & reach

141

Three from Two:

Bent
      like bow.   This is
the dream of the triangle.   Pyramid.
The Work
          crosses the first veil.   Sways
the double star.
          Draws space aside just
enough
    for the other to shine.
              As thru a pinprick
in a black curtain.
          Wind
against our hearts
          & we dance & know
again
    he is Other
          than fire.

& out of the Three
the Four, as One:

this is the Mystery of which we
are metaphor. Or the uni-
verse   4-square founded
stretched out on cross of matter
in the Light.
              Filtering colors   red
green   blue   & other
than the winds.
The elements are other than the winds.
& not so easily fooled.
              Placated.

This suspension
              of particles of time
in an emptiness.
              When have we known it
except alone?   & so it is
                & is not
Real
    to us.
        It is the root of love.
The four as one.

           I mirror
you
      whom you love   you   mirror
etc   & yet
           we spin binary
exquisite
      pure as a quasar.
              We are the
mystery of which
         this is metaphor
O breathe
      against my skin.

STUDIES IN LIGHT

claritas:

sun
     caught in dew
flashing
a   shapeliness
we stand outside of

candor:

light
     a chorus swelling
filling out
the contours of architecture
cathedral
palace
        theatre

lumen:

light
as a glyph that writes itself
over & over, on the face
of water, inscrutable
perpetual motion

lux:

needle point
moving out
from core
of earth
thinnest
piercing   rays

ARS METALLURGICA

A mystery of love lies concealed in the metal
—Robert Duncan

1.
beneath the skin of metals a total love is growing
untapped, except for the sighs of the *cenote*
crystals like teardrops toss in the underground waters
the fruits of the tree of metals

> that stretches horizontal
> close lover to the magnet
> presses its full length
> along the lines of force that like a skein
> enmesh the friable earth
> compact it

> for to grow horizontal
> from a seed
> of densest water
> is to call gravitation to account
> stretch limbs
> crosswise against the Belly of the world

the metals grow
w/their roots in underground streams
they grow horizontal
beneath the hide of the earth
resplendent, radiant Trees

2.
And the form of love of copper
specific
      of iron
clearly its own
tin too, & lead
like a wash of reassurance

we have all been made aware
of the loves of gold & silver
luna & sol to which our love
is drawn & the scintillating
intelligence of quicksilver
seduction of the grace of eternal
becoming.

        It becomes us
our delight
the metals bless us.

3.
(The play of them, they divide
& spread their limbs
        under the blanketing earth
they learn their songs
        each from the stream
in which it hath its beginning. . . .

NOTES ON *THE ART OF MEMORY*

for Thelonious Monk

The stars are a memory system
for thru them
                we remember our origin
Our home is behind the sun
or a divine wind
                that fills us
makes us think so.

DREAM POEM

there is a fire above the ramparts of the world
shaped like battlements, or like the hair
of Orcagna's women

there is a fire beyond the skin of the world
a fire burns behind the skin of the world

TO MY FATHER—2

You were dying of grief from the moment I saw you
Or fear, tho there *was* a slight chink
thru which we cd signal each other.
How many nights w/a pillow over my face
did I struggle w/rage / or desire
exhaustion. There are no fat gods
I thought then. Tho yr tears bloated
you & yr anger puffed you out.
There is Bes, the dwarf, but
I didn't know it then. I will not die
yr death. I will mourn but will not
join you in that house
you build away from the others.
I will know
the tower inside & out, the goddess
in the lingam. Orchards
which do not grow
on city roofs.   If only you'd lie down
to die in an orchard. Amaranth,
almond, even the feckless
acacia. You are dying of grief
on the rooftops / of yr mind, but things
grow in the ground.

"MY LOVER'S EYES
ARE NOTHING LIKE THE SUN"

for Sheppard

These eyes are amber, they
have no pupils, they are filled
w/a blue light (fire).
They are the eyes of gods
the eyes of insects, straying
godmen of the galaxy, metallic
wings.
            Those eyes were green
are still, sea green, or grey
their light
less defined.   These sea-green
eyes spin dreams on the
palpable air. They are not yrs
or mine. It is as if the dead
saw thru our eyes, others for a moment
borrowed these windows, gazing.
We keep still. It is as if these windows
filled for a minute w/a different
light.

Not blue, not amber. But the curtain drawn
over our daily gaze is drawn aside.
Who are you, really. I have seen it
often enough, the naked
gaze of power. We "charge"
the other with it / the leap
into non-betrayal, a wind
w/out sound we live in. Where
are we, really, climbing
the sides of buildings to peer in
like spiderman, at windows
not our own

THE DOCTRINE OF SIGNATURES

There are knowable numbers too
As when the primrose reveals the six in its heart
But the number imprinted on my heart
Is a darker business.

Say this: the pulse of pain
is a cycle of five.
                    And you have not said
all. The mighty wind
                    blows from the 8 to the 7
thru the Tower called God's house
                    What signature
shapes the vector of the breath
                    flowing outward?

There is a smoke that arises from the heart
a pillar of cloud of the Will
                    & we move toward the Good
like the stars, like young rams,   like a god
who yearns to be himself
                    & frighten no one.

HEADLANDS: THE MUSIC

what remains are the poppies
                         the daisies
growing in clumps
                    (the astral
light)
        Only here it is clear
pellucid   an embarrassment
                                here
"clear as a bell"   pitch
                         is performed in color
the pitch of the mountains
                         as they lean toward
the plain.   the spiky grasses
green & darkest
                         green which is purple
dappled light.   the clouds
                         dopplered
light   /   red shift
                         but there is no red
in this place.
                Only gold, the poppies
& clearest
            white (a *candor*)
                         color is
a language
                greenpurple grasses, the eye
moved again to these
                         they repeat for us
to decipher.   A language of flowers
of colors.
                A language of light

FOR BELLA AKHMADULINA

Note: In her great poem "I Swear",
written for her forerunner, the poet
Marina Tsvetaeva, Bella Akhmadulina
vows to "kill Yelabuga", the town in
which Tsvetaeva hanged herself in
1941. Akhmadulina addresses the town
as if it were some kind of malevolent
entity or demon.

A life for a life, a young black
woman's voice said to me on the
phone the day George
Jackson died in prison and I
said even twenty, a hundred for that
one would be cheap. Even a thousand.
And if I claimed a million
lives for each of my lost, like some
superHitler out to depopulate
the earth, and cd drink, somehow
that blood: this one's
for you, Freddie, and this for you,
Lee Probst, Genevieve, Gloria still
alive but dead and you, Little One
we called you & this immensity
of gore I drink to you, Jimmy, teacher
and friend. O lost mad Mike, killed brain of Timothy, palsy
in Allen's face, this one's
for Warren Miller, nobody knows
they killed. Fred Hampton in his bed, asleep
in blood. Emmett who told us
it wdn't be "overdose" that got him,

a million lives for each,
so what, it wd take four thousand only
to finish us all then & I alone
cd probably name four thousand.
Listen.
There's got to be another way, we can't
just kill *yelabuga* or be killed. Or both.
There's
anyway here, the ghost dance, or tin
floating as gold in the vessel. I know it's nonsense
but is it worse nonsense than drinking yourself to death
tonight in some Russian suburb? Here
we've got Black Elk's four horses in the sky
to replace the ones in Revelations. What
have you got? You must have *something*
I won't be "translated"
alone, or at least w/out female
buddies, I know some of the men will "buy" the ideal
but they don't count, they never carried their flesh
grave as lead, there must be a peasant whisper
the shape of a hill, or a sneaky look
in the eyes of an ancient icon—give me a hint
don't hide
& die,
        there isn't enough blood on earth
to buy our losses.   And blood is salt, it will never
quench my thirst.   Do we kill,
or split
        or kill & split
                        or translate this shit
to a paradise omitting nothing taking
w/us.   Gravid, full
of the squirming seeds of our dead

can we
sow the wind?

can we
condense fury till it is
flame
    can we use this fuel
to move us out of here,

                      a flying leap
to another "plane" or "sphere"
& I don't know into what, don't ask, only
I know it won't be *worse.*

PARACELSUS:

Extract the juice which is itself a Light.

Pulp, manna, gentle
        Theriasin, ergot
like mold on flame, these red leaves
bursting
        from mesquite by the side
of dry creekbed. Extract

the tar, the sticky
substance
      heart
            of things
(each plant a star, extract

the juice of stars
            by circular stillation
smear
     the inner man w/the coction
till he burn
     like worms of light in quicksilver
not the false
     puffballs of marshfire, extract

the heart of the empty heart
        it is full
of the star soul that paces fierce
in the deeps of earth
       the Red Man,
             healer
in furs
     who carries a club

who carries
          the pale homunculus
in his belly.
          For you are angel, you call
the soul from plants

          or pearls of ambergris
out of the grudging sea.
          Extract arcanum. Separate
true Archeus from the false
          the bitter
is not less potent—nor does clarity
bespeak truth.

          Out of the heart of the ineffable
draw the black flecks of matter
          & from these
the cold, blue fire.
          Dry water. Immerse
yourself
     though it be but a drop.
          This Iliaster
flowers like the wind.
     Out of the ash, the Eidolon of the world

Crystalline.
     Perfect.

JOHN DEE:

1.

Thru the transparency of water is the explication of light
This light is a mean toward the manifoldness of numbers
which are nothing but the implicit, infolded upon itself & transparent
This is the circle of the world, a perfect window of crystal

The clockwork of the heavens is a distortion of the transparent
pierced thru w/crystals & pinned to the unpresent sphere
which continuously unfolds like the rose in the center of the beehive
Leaving only the geometries of the mind, like the lens of the eye
Flickering in apparent alterations of the light

Tetrahedron delineates concavities of the Mirror

2.

Trifoliate the womb of the virgin
One door thru which verdigris & black in undetermined sequence
Abet the wolfhound who tracks us thru corners of the wood
The angles of dodecahedron enfolding the infinite maze
Like the hollow space in an egg, teeth of gears
that wind us back before the beginning, this perfection
was with him
                    at the creation of the world

3.

March of archangels, theophany
of implicate wings, dimensional
space yielding to space in a depth
that requires no sounding. Trace them
like frost on the glass our tears
make of the heavens

RANT

You cannot write a single line w/out a cosmology
a cosmogony
laid out, before all eyes

there is no part of yourself you can separate out
saying, this is memory, this is sensation
this is the work I care about, this is how I
make a living

it is whole, it is a whole, it always was whole
you do not "make" it so
there is nothing to integrate, you are a presence
you are an appendage of the work, the work stems from
hangs from the heaven you create

every man / every woman carries a firmament inside
& the stars in it are not the stars in the sky

w/out imagination there is no memory
w/out imagination there is no sensation
w/out imagination there is no will, desire

history is a living weapon in yr hand
& you have imagined it, it is thus that you
"find out for yourself"
history is the dream of what can be, it is
the relation between things in a continuum

of imagination
what you find out for yourself is what you select
out of an infinite sea of possibility
no one can inhabit yr world

yet it is not lonely,
the ground of imagination is fearlessness
discourse is video tape of a movie of a shadow play
but the puppets are in yr hand
your counters in a multidimensional chess
which is divination
                        & strategy

the war that matters is the war against the imagination
all other wars are subsumed in it.

the ultimate famine is the starvation
of the imagination

it is death to be sure, but the undead
seek to inhabit someone else's world

the ultimate claustrophobia is the syllogism
the ultimate claustrophobia is "it all adds up"
nothing adds up & nothing stands in for
anything else

THE ONLY WAR THAT MATTERS IS THE WAR AGAINST
                                THE IMAGINATION
THE ONLY WAR THAT MATTERS IS THE WAR AGAINST
                                THE IMAGINATION
THE ONLY WAR THAT MATTERS IS THE WAR AGAINST
                                THE IMAGINATION

ALL OTHER WARS ARE SUBSUMED IN IT

There is no way out of the spiritual battle
There is no way you can avoid taking sides
There is no way you can *not* have a poetics
no matter what you do: plumber, baker, teacher

you do it in the consciousness of making
or not making yr world
you have a poetics: you step into the world
like a suit of readymade clothes

or you etch in light
your firmament spills into the shape of your room
the shape of the poem, of yr body, of yr loves

A woman's life / a man's life is an allegory

Dig it

There is no way out of the spiritual battle
the war is the war against the imagination
you can't sign up as a conscientious objector

the war of the worlds hangs here, right now, in the balance
it is a war for this world, to keep it
a vale of soul-making

the taste in all our mouths is the taste of our power
and it is bitter as death

bring yr self home to yrself, enter the garden
the guy at the gate w/the flaming sword is yrself

the war is the war for the human imagination
and no one can fight it but you/ & no one can fight it for you

The imagination is not only holy, it is precise
it is not only fierce, it is practical
men die everyday for the lack of it,
it is vast & elegant

intellectus means "light of the mind"
it is not discourse it is not even language
the inner sun

the *polis* is constellated around the sun
the fire is central

PHOSPHOROS

*Watch carefully that you may see the Day-star
arising with deliverance. . .*

— *Philalethes*

The morning star casts light on all
the towers on the hill.

We consort w/angels
We are the prey of beings
who break us open to extract the seed
The mineral sperm which flows
      like vapor from our hearts

There is no quarter in this war against
      our outdated humanity
We set our feet on our own heads
      & climb

to the beloved & wrathful form, the female form
of what man could be
fluid and cold as starlight.

Precise as mathematics

*"The sky was green as morning
      & the dew
lay golden on the grass."*

SWALLOW SEQUENCE

[the swallows' nest was removed
from the shrine tent: "it is hoped
they will procreate elsewhere."]

1
after hearing us take the precepts
the swallows decided
it was safe to nest in the Shrine Tent

2
we have removed the nests
and now—
what will we tell the Lohans?

3
when their new eggs hatch
these swallows will teach their young
that Buddhists, like all humans
are not to be trusted

ANOTHER REVOLUTIONARY LETTER, 1988

(Gestapo Poem)

Where is gestapo, where
does it end? Where
is it? Soweto, it is. Where
does it end? Not
Oakland, it doesn't
not B'nai Brith.

Where
is it? Gaza, it is. Where
is it? San Quentin, it is. Where?
Peru. Where? Paris. Where? in Bonn
& Prague & Beijing, it is
in Yellow River Valley. Where
is it? Afghan, Guatemala, Rio,
Alaska, Tierra del Fuego, the
wasted taiga, it is
where is it?
& where
does it end.
          Not in
Oakland, it doesn't,
not in London. Not in the Mission.
Don't end in Brooklyn
or Rome. Atlanta. Where?
Morocco, gestapo is
Sudan (& death)
Where end? not Canada sold to
Nazi USA
not Mexico, Kenya, Australia
it don't, not end
Jamaica, Haiti. Mozambique
not end. Maybe
someplace it isn't maybe

someplace it ends
some hills maybe
still free
        but hungry
                (eyes
blaze
     over ancient guns

Poems from

LOBA

AVE

O lost moon sisters
crescent in hair, sea underfoot do you wander
in blue veil, in green leaf, in tattered shawl do you wander
with goldleaf skin, with flaming hair do you wander
on Avenue A, on Bleecker Street do you wander
on Rampart Street, on Fillmore Street do you wander
with flower wreath, with jeweled breath do you wander

    footprints
          shining mother of pearl
               behind you
   moonstone eyes
      in which the crescent moon

with gloves, with hat, in rags, in fur, in beads
under the waning moon, hair streaming in black rain
wailing with stray dogs, hissing in doorways
shadows you are, that fall on the crossroads, highways

jaywalking do you wander
spitting do you wander
mumbling and crying do you wander
aged and talking to yourselves
with roving eyes do you wander
hot for quick love do you wander
weeping your dead

       naked you walk
       swathed in long robes you walk
       swaddled in death shroud you walk
       backwards you walk

             hungry
             hungry
             hungry

shrieking I hear you
singing I hear you
cursing I hear you
praying I hear you

you lie with the unicorn
you lie with the cobra
you lie in the dry grass
you lie with the yeti
you flick long cocks of satyrs with your tongue

you are armed
you drive chariots
you tower above me
you are small
you cower on hillsides
out of the winds

pregnant you wander
barefoot you wander
battered by drunk men you wander

you kill on steel tables
you birth in black beds
fetus you tore out stiffens in snow
it rises like new moon
you moan in your sleep

digging for yams you wander
looking for dope you wander
playing with birds you wander
chipping at stone you wander

I walk the long night seeking you
I climb the sea crest seeking you
I lie on the prairie, batter at stone gates
calling your names

you are coral
you are lapis and turquoise
your brain curls like shell
you dance on hills

    hard-substance-woman you whirl
    you dance on subways
    you sprawl in tenements
    children lick at your tits

you are the hills, the shape and color of mesa
you are the tent, the lodge of skins, the hogan
the buffalo robes, the quilt, the knitted afghan
you are the cauldron and the evening star
you rise over the sea, you ride the dark

I move within you, light the evening fire
I dip my hand in you and eat your flesh
you are my mirror image and my sister
you disappear like smoke on misty hills
you lead me thru dream forest on horseback
large gypsy mother, I lean my head on your back

I am you
and I must become you
I have been you
and I must become you
I am always you
I must become you

    ay-a
    ay-a ah
    ay-a
    ay-a ah ah
    maya ma maya ma
    om star mother ma om
    maya ma ah

LOVE SONG OF THE LOBA

O my lord, blue beast
on the pale green snows, see
I have been running to keep up
w / you
        I have been
                running to find you
my tongue
        scours ice your
                tracks made
I drink
      hollows of yr steps,
                I thought
many a dark beast was you only to find
perfume of your fur, bright cloud
of yr breath not there, they are
flesh & clay, heavy dross, they do not
fly
  in the wind,
          see I have flown
to you, do you
        lurk in night
            do you sail
to sea on an ice floe
         howling sacred songs

O my lord, my good
        dark beast
           how is it
I cannot taste you
        wraith & shadow
tripleheaded
      blind god of my
          spirit, you burn

blue flame on the
              green ice, long shadows
lick at yr eyes
          yr fur like arctic night
                   the fire
of your song

I will circle the earth,
             I will circle the
                       wheeling stars
keening, my blue gems
            shoot signals
                to yr heart:
I am yr loved one, lost from eternity
                  I am
yr *śakti*
      wheeling thru
            black space
I, the white wolf,
          Loba,
            call to you
blue mate,
      O lost lord
            of the failing hills

THE LOBA CONTINUES TO SING

I will make you flesh again
(have you slipped away)
think you to elude, become past
& black & white
as photographs,
                    O I will
lure you into being till you stand
flesh solid against my own
                    I will spread my hair
over yr feet
                    my tongue
shall give you shape, I will
make you flesh & carry you
away, O bright
black lord you are, & I
your sister
                    & magic carpet

Will you ride?

*   *   *

O I tumbled here for you, I put on flesh
drew down this skull over my flaming light
          slipped on this shaggy pelt
to make it easy for yr spirit to speak to mine

As in that bright unclouded ocean where the stars
are not yet born, where you & I
slid, tumbling like dolphins
                              we cd not
speak each other's names,

          O you leaped
into the worlds, & I followed
did I not
          falling & shrieking
I solidified.
          Merely to look, my lord
once more
into your great
                    sad beast eyes

Share this sorrow.

SOME LIES ABOUT THE LOBA

that she is eternal, that she sings
that she is star-born, that she gathers crystal
that she can be confused with Isis
that she is the goal
that she knows her name, that she swims
in the purple sky, that her fingers are pale & strong

that she is black, that she is white
that you always know who she is
when she appears
that she strides on battlements, that she sifts
like stones in the sea
that you can hear her approach, that her jewelled feet
tread any particular measure

that there is anything about her
which cannot be said
that she relishes tombstones, falls
down marble stairs
that she is ground only, that she is not ground
that you can remember the first time you met
that she is always with you
that she can be seen without grace

that there is anything to say of her
which is not truth

LOBA AS EVE

I am Thou & Thou art I
and where Thou art I am
and in all things am I dispersed

and from wherever Thou willst
Thou gatherest Me

but in gathering Me
Thou Gatherest Thyself

—*Gospel of Eve*

where tossing in grey sheets you weep
I am
where pouring like mist you
                              scatter among the stars
I shine
where in black oceans of sea & sky
            you die
            you die
I chant
a voice like angels from the heart
of virgin gold,
              plaint of the unicorn caught
in the boundless circle

              where you confront
broken glass, lost trees & men
                        tossed up
on my beaches, hear me pray:
                          your words
slip off my tongue, I am pearl
of yr final tears, none other
than yr flesh, though it go soft

I am worm
            in the tight bud, burst
of starcloud that covers your dream & morning
I am sacred mare grazing
            in meadow of yr spirit & you run
in my wind. Hear the chimes
that break from my eyes like infants
struggling eternally against
                        these swaddling clothes

and where Thou art, I am

astride the wind. or held
by two hoodlums under a starting truck.
crocheting in the attic.
striding forever out of the heart of quartz
immense, unhesitant, monotonous
as galaxies; or rain; or
lost cities of the dinosaurs now sunk
in the unopening rock.

who keeps the bats from flying in your window?
who rolls the words you drop back into seed?
                          who picks
sorrows like lice from your heart & cracks them
                          between her teeth?
who else blows down your chimney with the moon
scattering ashes from your dismal hearth to show
the sleeping Bird in the coals, or is it
garnet you lost?

              What laughter spins you
around in the windy street?

& in all things am I dispersed

gold fleece on the hunted deer.
the Name of everything.
sweet poison eternally churned
from the milky ocean.
futurity's mirror.   ivory gate
of death.
the fruit I hold out spins
the dharma wheel.
I weep
I weep
dry water I am, cold fire, "our"
Materia, mother & matrix
                    eternally in labor.
The crescent I stand on rocks
like a shaky boat, it is
the winking eye of God.

& from wherever Thou willst
Thou gatherest Me

steel, from the belly of Aries.
Or that cold fire which plays
above the sea.
White sow munching acorns in graveyards where roots
of oaks wrap powdery bones of the devas.
There, suckle at my tits. Crucify
me like a beetle on yr desk. Nod out
amidst the rustling play of lizards, recognize
epics the lichen whisper, read twigs
& leaves as they fall.

Nurture my life with quartz & alabaster
& drink my blood from a vein in my lower leg.
I neigh, I nuzzle you, I explode
                your certain myth.
I crawl slimy from a cave beneath yr heart
I hiss, I spit oracles at yr front door
in a language you have forgotten. I unroll
the scroll of yr despair, I bind yr children with it.

It is for this you love me.
It is for this
you seek me everywhere.

Because I gave you apples out of season
Because I gnaw at the boundaries of the light

but in gathering Me
Thou Gatherest Thyself

daystar that hovers
over the heavy waters of that Sea
bright stone that fell
out of the fiery eye of the pyramid

it grows
out of the snake as out of the crescent:
apple you eternally devour
forever in your hand. I lock
the elements around you where you walk:

> earth from my terror
> water from my grief
> air my eternal flight
> & fire / my lust

I am child who sings
uninjured in the furnace of your flesh.

Blue earth am I & never on this earth
have I been naked
Blue light am I that runs
like marrow in the thin line of yr breath

I congeal
waterlilies on the murky pond
I hurl
the shafts of dawn like agony
                              down the night

SONG OF HELOISE

from out of the body of fire,
            the body of light
out of the wind, *virtù*

the light that is in the mind
these essences
moving
            pale color
al fresco
            a homecoming   (clarities
from out of the passion
            crystal, spiralling

books open within the Word
                        small windows
light within light
            "space is a
                        lotus"

from the body of light
                        like dayspring
ineffable breath

& out of the crystal,
                  the fountain
                              jets like sperm
quintessence

            how the flesh
            adheres
                in its
                passing

THE LOBA RECOVERS
THE MEMORY OF A MARE

small hooves
the ankles fragile
unsteady
not rooted here

the eyes
anxious
eyes of a doe
who has been hunted
but not w/in recent
memory

who walked across America behind gaunt violent yogis
& died o-d'ing in methadone jail
scarfing the evidence

or destitute in Fiji wiring home for comfort
destroyed among oil lamps Morocco seeking dead fingers
old man in Afghani jail / pregnant barefoot & whoring
        who did we pray
        who did we pray to then

laid out flowerless in abandoned basement
blue stiff & salt injection
just out of reach

wrote lipstick "save yourself" on tin rail of furnished
        room bed
eloped w/white slaver & died Indiana of unmentioned griefs
or in love again peaceful scrawled candlesmoke "there is
        salvation" triumphant on borrowed ceiling
while friends coughed in the kitchen

who left tapestries, evidence, baby bottle behind in Vancouver
& hitched to Seattle for the mushroom season
trailing welfare checks & stolen money orders
Chicago gangster in earrings who minded the baby

who gathered reed grass for the wicki-up, eating
      horsemeat steaks in Colorado dusk
the painted hills bucking & neighing, it was her ankles

    were slender
    it was her eyes
    were tired

oatmeal & grits while the old man
      naked in bed / read Bible / jerked off
& who was the whore of Babylon in the
      kerosene lamp of yr childhood?

it was her skirt
was greasy
it was her skirt
was graceful
it was her skirt
you clung to, till she fell
you fell

     & who now remembers her hands
working dye into cotton
slant of her green eyes / Sagamore cafeteria

who has tears for girls now on Route One, the babies
wrapped in a scarf / the green
        always further north
        further than you can walk

    her ankles fragile
    unrooted, she walks
    into the Wind

THE LOBA ADDRESSES THE GODDESS / OR THE POET AS PRIESTESS ADDRESSES THE LOBA-GODDESS

Is it not in yr service that I wear myself out
running ragged among these hills, driving children
to forgotten movies? In yr service
broom & pen. The monstrous feasts
we serve the others on the outer porch
(within the house there is only rice & salt)
And we wear exhaustion like a painted robe
I & my sisters
                    wresting the goods from the niggardly
                            dying fathers
healing each other w / water & bitter herbs

that when we stand naked in the circle of lamps
(beside the small water, in the inner grove)
we show
no blemish, but also no superfluous beauty.
It has burned off in watches of the night.
O Nut, O mantle of stars, we catch at you
        lean   mournful
      ragged   triumphant
          shaggy as grass
our skins ache of emergence / dark o' the moon

THE SECOND DAUGHTER: Li (Brightness)

You enter power, but I am here before you
standing in what's left of grace on this planet
the bits shored up, to form a circle of light
I cannot abdicate, even for you
            come, join us!

You enter womanhood, I am a woman
to greet you, invest you, praise you
(there are oils for your skin, your hair)
I have not grown old suddenly before yr eyes
        have not the courtesy to be decrepit
            small
        in the wind at my back & yrs
I have dances still to dance—do you dance?
        how the lights
        dance in you, eyes & skin
                    & brights of yr hair
How yr anger dances!

See how my skin
            like yrs
                    takes on its sheen
after lovemaking
                    see how we glow!

The circle which is a spiral
stretches out
                to the star of Isis
it is the stair of Light
                in the upper parts glow
the Grandmothers
            laughing

The Ancestress reaches her hand
to draw us up.
        She is white vulture
          w/ spiral neck

    These years are the windings
of Light
    our flesh flickers & changes
like flame.
    Like flame, it holds us fast.

"APPARUIT"

There is some sweet woman
whose words I have never seen
who springs
fullblown into mind

It is as if she had printed a large book
& her work was full & satisfied
& she
satisfied in the loves of both sexes
not strung out

by the *rappel á l'ordre*
not straining
or excusing herself or defiant
strident angry
not pushed out of shape

She has moved gracefully from fleshly maidenhood
to the lean delights of the mother

she is serene
with the grace & gentleness of the warrior
the spear
the harp the book the butterfly
are equal
in her hands

There is a woman who is full of grace
her lap is ample & empty
she is not abstract or sheepish
there are no tendons
straining in her neck

her voice is not milk & honey
it is not harsh, it is a voice
her voice   she writes

whatever suits her   she moves
where she pleases   she casts
a variable shadow

There is a woman whose poems are bread & meat
hyacinth   nightmare   crêpe paper
crab nebula

I close a window, she is not reflected in it
but I see her silhouette against the glass

she is crisp as ice, is soft
as russian vowels

O sweet whore innocent
power my fiend
perfect fraud
you essence sniffing
my hand   yr inner ear
is the acoustic chamber
of stars
you commit
this poem like a ripe plum
I devour here in a desert
whose fountain   no caravans
stream toward

O shadow sister!

DEER LEAP

for Robert Duncan

1.

High hart at deer leap, park
to forest, the Law
changes utterly, rupture
of plane.   High hart moves sideways
across the path, her spoor
smells of fear, wind leaps
the deer leap, the law
in the park, formal, composed,
treacherous.   Who goes forth
to return?   Wind
from the quarters spirals
in on itself.   The hart
fox or wolf, the beast
of the forest, sacred wood
                          spins
spirals or spins to a destiny
or brook, no hart can leap
over.   There drinks
reflecting.   Still.

2.

Wonder is light
at wood's edge, falling
reflecting green, wonder
is open space where the forest
closes itself, and nothing
protects or shelters.
Outside the forest, no law
shelters the beast of the wood.

No law outside   where wonder
sings limpid, glances
sideways. Let us go then
love, where light
twinkles in the gap
between the Law
& ourselves.

3.
Darkling he follows.   It is as fox
or marten, his eyes are,
                    he has eyes
for the black green under leaves
in the small moon.   It shimmers
phosphorus, fungus,   the low
shift in the grass.   Dark he goes
into the light,   a flat
bent shadow it is joy
to see on the grass.   Come
love,   what slivers fall
like flakes of light from a burning
tower they catch
in yr hair yr smile.   Winter
slips between our clasping
hands

4.
Do we break cover,   break
thru the small grass,   bracken
is there light off the tall rocks
they stand far on the plain.   We slip
from plain to plane, not daring
to turn back, we are far
from the white stair

                    what yr words
cannot say,   my tears
do not buy,   cuts a swathe
like the hare
            in tall grass
under the moon
                  we totter
aside to leap again
                  that hedge
or pass thru gate,   same flat
plain on either side
but the Laws   are different.

5.
sly as a marten,   evade
natural law   replace
one boundary w/another, we flow
to its edge,   roll back
define   this pain as content
rest-
        less as wind,   renew
ingathering,   to leap

sly as the shy
fox, remember, no law
protects the hare
                  from park
to wood to common
land he slips
            always at risk
& always
        kin to the moon

6.
whisper my name, little Brother, whisper
across the Net that links the stars
                    where yr angel
buzzes like an insect, hovers,
                the Rose
gives honey to the bees, not cunt
        not heart or christ, *rose*
is the soul,   yr soul
the angels suck at.   Oh love
light   displaced   making room
where gaps in the old
law
        flow like melting ice

7.
let us be what we are,   mid leap
let us fall or rise
on the breath the Will
                    yields to.
there are eyes
under all the leaves,   there are
lynxes, yes
            & the whisper
of passing shadow, but wonder
is there where boundary
breaks against itself
                & the Law
shivers & bursts like diamonds
                in the heart

PARTHENOS

the black stone shines tho its
color / clarity   we cannot
do not   name   & the door
swings soundless   hingeless as the
panel in his skull
                    who enclosed
claimed the war goddess
                              she who was
Owl in Africk   before
Zeus came out of the ground

The black stone
                    whose
clearness /   we dare not
enter   emits   a light
& the door swings   soundless
inviting   *its* light
is golden
            we know this tho the stone remains
inscrutable &

soft as the stone in
                    toad's head
Hekāt
          frog-goddess   in what
was later
          Zulu

She who heals   thru darkness.

He enclosed   Durga, armed
maiden,   cast her forth   his
headache   whose armies march
chthonic   whose destruction
takes place under ground
                          & she rose
feathers on her shoulders, a shadow
long as the road:
               "Athena. New beginnings."

Now death is in the light
                          it is
the light   golden   the door
soundless   the path   a silhouette
or outline of the Bird
the Owl, Hawk   all those
whose beak curves downward

Storms are bred underground   the sky
Revealer,   the
Interpreter   of what moves
in the earth.   Our dead
in the light of day
                    primary
lyke before the sun
                    is created
rises   our Dead disperse
on the wind
            as the hairs
of her feathers   move
her feathered shield.

First light is lightning   "worms"
dart thru the void   the arrows
before the storm
                    we aver / the Raveler
whose helmet
                 crests in plumes
a black wind
                 flows out of them
brings pestilence
                    the light
at her back
            the male-born
woman,   outlined
                    black   definite

the path   she sd   is the body
of the god
            / dess
                  The death
she carries golden suffused
inviting—her field is the
entrance point   the door
emits a mist
                  miasm

pharmakos
            is the stone   it glints
green / golden / black
Her feathered skull   Athena
New
       Beginnings.

Diane di Prima Chronology

1934—Born in Brooklyn. Maternal grandfather, Domenico Mallozzi, an Anarchist and friend of Carlo Tresca, was a strong influence.

1948—Entered Hunter High School in Manhattan. Made lifelong commitment to poetry.

1951—Studied one and a half years at Swarthmore College.

1953—Moved to Lower East Side to write and study. Corresponded with Pound and Patchen.

1955—Visited Ezra Pound at St. Elizabeth's Hospital daily for two weeks. Stayed with his companion, the painter Sheri Martinelli.

1956—Corresponded with Ferlinghetti and Ginsberg. Met choreographer and teacher James Waring and began to study with him: Zen, random techniques, meditative composition.

1957—Met Ginsberg, Kerouac, Orlovsky, and Corso in New York. Birth of first daughter, Jeanne.

1958—First book of poems published: *This Kind of Bird Flies Backwards.*

1959—Stage managed Monday night series for James Waring at the Living Theatre.

1960—First book of prose, *Dinners and Nightmares,* published by Corinth Press.

1961—With co-editor LeRoi Jones (Amiri Baraka), began *The Floating Bear,* a mimeographed newsletter. With Fred Herko, LeRoi Jones, Alan Marlowe and James Waring, founded New York Poets Theatre, which produced four seasons of one-act plays by poets, with fine-arts sets by New York and West Coast painters. On trip to West Coast met Robert Duncan, George Herms, Michael McClure, Kirby Doyle, and Wallace Berman. Arrested with LeRoi Jones by FBI for alleged obscenity of the *Bear;* case thrown out by grand jury.

1962—Birth of second daughter, Dominique, whose father is LeRoi Jones. Met Shunryu Suzuki Roshi in San Francisco and began study with him. Married Alan Marlowe.

1963—Birth of first son, Alexander. LeRoi Jones resigned from co-editorship of *The Floating Bear.* Poets Theatre (together with Jonas Mekas' Cinematheque) implicated in an obscenity case involving Jean Genet's film, *Chant d'Amour;* ensuing long civil rights suits eventually won.

1964—With Alan Marlowe, founded Poets Press, which published first books by Audre Lorde, David Henderson, Clive Matson, Herbert Huncke, and others. Death by suicide of close friend and confrère, the dancer and choreographer Fred Herko.

1965—Poets Theatre closed. Moved to Rammurti Mishra's ashram in Monroe, New York.

1966—Moved to Kerhonkson, New York, and later to Timothy Leary's experimental community at Millbrook, New York.

1967—Twenty thousand mile trip around USA in VW bus, read at discotheques, bars, storefronts, universities, galleries. Birth of third daughter, Tara.

1968—Moved to San Francisco. Worked with the Diggers for a year and a half, distributing free food. *Revolutionary Letters* are widely published by the underground press. Began close study with Suzuki at Zen Center.

1969—Death of father. Divorced from Alan Marlowe. Studied at Tassajara Zen Mountain Center.

1970—Met Chogyam Trungpa Rinpoche at Tassajara. Birth of second son, Rudi.

1971—Began six years of teaching for Poetry in the Schools, mostly in Wyoming, Montana, Arizona and Minnesota: reform schools, reservations, prisons. Taught women's writing workshop for Zen Center community. Began long poem, *Loba*.

1972—Disaffiliated from Zen Center. Married Grant Fisher. Founded Eidolon Editions, and published *The Calculus of Variation*. Began writing, visualization, and dream workshops at Intersection for the Arts, which continued through 1975.

1973—Moved to Marshall, California, near Point Reyes.

1974—Taught at opening session of Poetics Program at the Naropa Institute in Boulder, Colorado.

1975—Produced *Whale Honey*, a full-length play, in San Francisco and Los Angeles. Divorced Grant Fisher.

1976—Founded The Poets Institute, a community graphics and typesetting center, in Point Reyes. Received Arts-in-Social-Institutions fellowship from California Arts Council to teach writing and collage at Napa State Hospital. Birth of grandson, Christopher. First trip to Europe, for Rotterdam Poetry Festival.

1977—Met Sheppard Powell. Taught local workshops in Point Reyes.

1978—Returned to San Francisco and studied psychic reading with Helen Palmer. Published *Loba, Parts 1-8*. Taught at The Neighborhood Foundation. Co-founded The Gold Circle, a group of artists interested in meditation, visualization and magical practice. Birth of granddaughter, Chani.

1980—Established Masters Program in Poetics at New College of California (with Robert Duncan, Duncan McNaughton, David Meltzer, and Louis Patler.) Taught hermetic traditions in poetry there through 1987. Studied healing with Greg Schelkun.

1981—Began working privately as psychic and healer.

1983—Began formal study with Chogyam Trungpa. Founded San Francisco Institute of Magical and Healing Arts (with Janet Carter, Carl Grundberg, and Sheppard Powell).

1985—Death of mother.
1983 to present—Writing and teaching at San Francisco Institute of Magical and Healing Arts. Continuing to study and practice Tibetan Buddhism, as well as magic, alchemy, and healing.

Works in progress: *Alchemical Fragments* (poetry); *Not Quite Buffalo Stew* (satirical novel); *Recollections of My Life as a Woman* (autobiographical memoir); and two critical studies; *Shelley: A Personal View*, and *The Mysteries of Vision* (about H.D.).

Index of Titles

202

Index of First Lines

16554

695
6